***conversations
on
counselling***

edited by
Marcus Lefébure

conversations on counselling

between a doctor and a priest

dialogue and trinity

edited by
Marcus Lefébure O.P.

T. & T. CLARK LIMITED
EDINBURGH

First published in Great Britain, 1982 by
T. & T. Clark Limited, 36 George Street,
Edinburgh EH2 2LQ.

ISBN: 0 567 29112 X

Printed by W.M. Bett Limited, Tillicoultry

Photo Typesetting by Swanston & Associates, Derby, England.

To
our friends

contents

acknowledgements

Grateful acknowledgement from the author is made to the following publishers for the use of material from their publications: Anthroposophic Press Inc., for a quotation from Rudolph Steiner: *Knowledge of the Higher Worlds* (pp 32-33, New York, 1947) and *Practical Training in Thought* (p. 13, New York, 1948); J.M. Dent & Sons Limited for a quotation from R.C. Zaehner: *Hindu Scriptures* (pp 67-68, Everyman Library, London, 1966); Eyre and Spottiswode for a passage from St. Thomas Aquinas: *Summa Theologica Volume 7* (p. 95, Andover, 1976); Rupert Hart-Davis for a quotation from Laurence Whistler: *The Initials in the Heart* (p. 234, London, 1966); Mosaik Verlag for a quotation from Udo Reiter: *Meditation — Wege zum Selbst* (p. 47, Munich, 1976); Princeton University Press for a quotation from Jolande Jacobi and R.F.C. Hull (Eds.): *C.G. Jung: Psychological Reflections: An Anthology* (p. 71, Princeton, 1953); Routledge and Kegan Paul for quotations from the English Edition of Jolande Jacobi and R.F.C. Hull (Eds): *C.G. Jung: Psychological Reflections: An Anthology* and also Hermann J. Weigand (Translator and Editor): *Goethe: Wisdom and Experience, Selections by Ludwig Curtius* (p. 164, London 1949); Verlag Urachhaus for a section from Hermann Beckh: *Der Hingang des Vollendeten* (p. 44, Stuttgart, 1960).

Was ist herrlicher als Gold? fragte der König. —
Das Licht, antwortete die Schlange. —
Was ist erquicklicher als Licht? fragte jener.—
Das Gespräch, antwortete diese.

(What is more glorious than gold? asked the king. —
The splendour of light, answered the serpent. —
What is more delectable than light? asked the former. —
The communion of dialogue, answered the latter. —)

Goethe Das Märchen

prologue

The air is thick with counselling: the term, the need, the call and the training for it. It was not always so; it was not so, say, some thirty years ago. Counselling is, therefore, still a very young discipline. At the same time it is coming of age fast. Indications of this are the publication in the immediate past alone of such books as the following: *Introduction to Psychotherapy* by D. Brown and J. Pedder (1979), which is a highly competent and authoritative mapping of the whole field of psychotherapy and the location of counselling within that field; *The Art of Psychotherapy* by Anthony Storr (1979), which seeks to articulate the factors common to the hitherto varied practice of depth-analysis over the past eighty years or so and then to make these available to the distinct but related field of psychotherapy; *Coding the Therapeutic Process: Emblems of Encounter* by Murray Cox (1978), sub-titled *A Manual for Counsellors and Therapists* and which is a reassessment of therapy. All such books therefore testify to the fact that counselling is becoming a discipline that can reflect critically upon itself. In other words, counselling is beginning to come to that maturity which consists in awareness of its own boundaries.

Just because counselling is thus both a young discipline but also one that is already beginning to become aware of its own boundaries, however, there has not been enough time for the development of those cross-disciplinary reflections and especially the sort of comparative discussion that brings about a consideration of the deeper presuppositions and values of the disciplines involved. It is one such discussion at the confines of two disciplines that we offer here. And it is a discussion in a full sense: it is a consideration but one that is shared; it is a reflection that is shared between a representative of one of the oldest relevant disciplines, that of the priesthood, as well as a representative of the young discipline of counselling itself; and it is presented in a series of

1

dialogues in order to emphasise by its very form the exploratory character of the inquiry.

Now this form is something that seemed to grow as organically as everything else represented in this book. Even on reflection, however, it did also seem to be the form that was most appropriate to the enterprise at the present stage in development of counselling. To presume to compare a little thing with a great, it was just this dialogue form that was chosen by St. Anselm at what proved to be the beginning of the renaissance of sustained thinking after the long night of the 'dark ages'. In his *Cur Deus Homo,* written about 1097, St. Anselm wrote tellingly: 'And since investigations that are conducted by way of question and answer are clearer and more agreeable to most people and especially to the slower spirits, I shall take as my interlocutor one of those who presses me with particular insistence, and so Boso will inquire and Anselm will reply'. And it must have been quite consciously that St. Anselm was renewing a perhaps even greater tradition, that of Plato's dialogues which capture for all time the genetic moment of subsequent European thinking.

Be this justification as it may, the dialogue form is the one we have chosen. And in order to catch the imaginative context and feel of these dialogues which my friend Dr. Gregory and I venture to present here, you have to picture to yourself an at first sight rather unlikely encounter — between, on the one hand, a short, stocky, largely bald man with bright, penetrating, animated eyes, an experienced paediatrician and counsellor in his late sixties and therefore now in semi-retirement, speaking with a broken, mid-European accent, somebody at once sharp and wise, and in this way revealing his Jewish background, and, on the other hand, a slim, bearded, alternately still and vivacious man some twenty years his junior, a Catholic priest speaking standard B.B.C. English except for his crumpled R. This last is the give-away; the defective R betrays at once his Austrian parentage and thereby also one important factor in the deep sympathy that had developed over the years between the two men. For Dr. Gregory had been born and brought up and done his medical studies in the same Vienna where my parents had been born and brought up, albeit on different sides of that Jewish world which had also nourished the young Freud. We had soon discovered this point in common after we had been introduced to each other by one of my confrères. In this way a contact which had begun by being professional soon became a deep personal friendship expressed in a series of fairly regular meetings over *Kaffee mit Schlag*, provided by Dr. Gregory's wife Emma. Thus the only adequate term for these meetings as they developed was Dr. Gregory's: each meeting was a *Gespräch*, a profound and mutually enriching encounter of feelings, thought and talk.

It was in the context of these soon fairly regular meetings over the years, in Dr. Gregory's simply furnished but book-lined study overlooking the hills to which my eyes could wander and rest meditatively, that the idea was first conceived and then gradually realised of devoting at least some of these conversations to topics of common concern and of recording them, at least for ourselves. Could we not explore together some of the deeper issues underlying the practice of counselling such as these emerged from our different but possibly complementary vantage points as counsellor and priest respectively? It was in this way that we devoted a number of, usually, Saturday mornings to such topics. We did not plan the whole series from the start but allowed the topics as it were to grow out of each other. Gradually, however, as these conversations and the discussions of their inter-relationship developed, a certain pattern suggested itself, and this is the pattern presented in the present book. The two pillars of the series, as Dr. Gregory had soon seen and so called them, are formed by the first and the fifth chapters on 'The Stages of Counselling' and 'The Stages of the Spiritual Path', which then developed into two corresponding sequels. These were then connected by two further chapters on 'Relationship and Solitude' and 'Woman and Man', whilst chapter 7 represents an after-thought of my own.

All these chapters (except the last) thus correspond to actual tape-recorded conversations and are broadly based on them in so far as they are edited versions of the latter. Further they all represent conversations between Dr. Gregory and myself, except the opening one, which was with another of Dr. Gregory's friends, a social worker whom we have called Bridget. This friend happened to ask Dr. Gregory about his practice of counselling a little before I asked him what in his opinion was involved in psychotherapy. What neither Bridget nor I realised until later was that we asked our questions at psychologically the ripe moment in Dr. Gregory's life

3

and so unwittingly precipitated a veritable *prise de conscience* or taking stock. And it is because the discussion with his friend the social worker was in so many ways more complete than the one Dr. Gregory had with me on the same subject a little later that we have preferred to include this as the opening dialogue rather than the similar one he had with me.

These conversations are, therefore, taken very much from life. In this connection, I should perhaps add a clarification. Dr. Gregory's observations are very much his own but their formulation takes on a colouring not entirely his own. The reason for this pertains to his very ability as a counsellor. He has the trained gift of entering into his interlocutor's world to the point of adjusting his language and approach to him. This was so between us. I am, therefore, convinced that had I been, not a Catholic priest but, say, an educationalist or a Buddhist, he would have couched his remarks otherwise. Not that the substance would have changed but only the terminology.

With these preliminary explanations, we now offer these conversations to a wider public in the hope that the spirit of mutual and common exploration in an atmosphere of personal trust and sympathy will kindle many more such encounters, *Gespräche*.

dialogue 1: the stages of counselling

'I'm really interested to know how you prepare for your counselling sessions, Martin', Bridget began. 'Working in the Social Work Department as I do, I get the impression that people don't take time to prepare themselves for these sessions and that they don't realise how important it is. I wonder how you feel about this?'

'Well', replied Dr. Gregory, 'I feel it is extremely important to *prepare*, and to prepare in a number of ways. First of all, I think it is very important to be aware of the fact that your general way of life is fundamental to successful counselling. And by "general way of life" I mean two distinct, though related, things. On the one hand, I think it is very important that the counsellor should have an all-round experience of human beings. In this connection I often think of a statement by Jüng. It is to be found in a collection of his sayings collected by one of his disciples, Jolande Jacobi, and it goes as follows:

> "The man who would learn the human mind will gain almost nothing from experimental psychology. Far better for him to put away his academic gown, to say good-bye to the study, and to wander with human heart through the world. There, in the horrors of the prison, the asylum and the hospital, in the drinking-shops, brothels, and gambling halls, in the salons of the elegant, in the exchanges, socialist meetings, churches, religious revivals, and sectarian ecstasies, through love and hate, through the experience of passions in every form in his own body, he would reap richer stores of knowledge than text-books a foot thick could give him. Then would he known how to doctor the sick with real knowledge of the human soul". [1]

On the other hand the counsellor should also have a balanced,

5

disciplined, rather serene way of life. For example, I think it would be very disturbing if I allowed myself to indulge in a great deal of social gossip and uncontrolled talk or watch a television programme which lasts too long and so on. I could give you many more examples which show that the way of life is most important. This is the first thing which seems to me to be fundamental. In the more immediate sense, I think it is critical that you approach an interview in a relaxed state of mind and body, and also that you clear your mind of all personal feelings, thoughts and preoccupations. The whole interview should be approached almost in a state of innocence and complete receptivity, so that you can perceive without any hindrance what you encounter in your client.'

'How do you feel about work being handed on to you about a client? I'm thinking in terms of files or other background information. Do you use that in your preparation?', asked Bridget.

'No, I usually just glance at them because if I were to immerse myself in the study of these documents, I should be far too thoroughly conditioned and that, I think, is absolutely detrimental to the objective, that is to say the unbiased approach to a client and to the unbiased perception of what you meet. Very often, of course in actual fact you meet something quite different from what you have been told in advance. But I do refer to the documents after I have formed the first basic impressions. For instance, I then make up my mind whether I can agree with the diagnosis or not. But I should feel that my mind were being cluttered up with thoughts and conclusions which are anticipating results instead of organically experiencing facts, and this I should consider a fundamental failure of the whole counselling process. The counselling process should begin in a state of pure receptivity that is objectively open to all impressions as they come towards you in a purely human way and you should not think in terms of diagnostic concepts; you should experience the human being in every way as you find him.'

'So, after glancing at what you have been told about a client, you would put it all at the back of your mind and then start completely afresh, forming your own impressions? '

'Yes, I should not only put it at the back of my mind; I should put in out of my mind.'

'Could we then go on to talk about how you actually start your session, Martin?'

'Yes, that depends on whether I am seeing the client for the first time, or whether I have seen him before. If I am seeing him for the first time, I try to make him comfortable, in a very informal way. I take him into the book-lined study which is deliberately furnished very simply. There are no pieces of furniture which indicate a professional set-up.'

'You're expressing a very unusual concept when you say that the study is specially arranged in a way to avoid any sign of a consulting room. I get the impression that you think of counselling as a personal encounter between two people rather than as an encounter between a consultant and a patient?'

'Yes, I do', replied Dr Gregory. 'For me, counselling is fundamentally, or should be, a human encounter calculated to give the person help and guidance. I think a counsellor is in the first place a human being who is able, in terms of his experience, his humanity, his maturity, to give this help. He is certainly not a professional psychiatrist with specialised knowledge, because the client then feels that he is not met on a human level, is not understood on a human level, that he is, to put it very bluntly, a "clinical specimen".'

'It is interesting that you should use this comparison now, because I was thinking in terms of the medical profession, and how, when you go to a psychiatrist or doctor, you are taken over, you think of yourself as being ill.'

'Yes. The client should not feel that he is scrutinised, that he is subjected to tests, that he is being cross-examined, but that he is simply met by another human being whom he can trust, to whom he can unburden himself and who, he hopes, may be able to help. Therefore, you see, everything that indicates professionalism is deliberately avoided, whilst everything that indicates a quiet, orderly, warm, human situation is gently emphasised. There are books in the room which give a thoughtful atmosphere, there are flowers which I always need in order to keep cheerful. The client's seat is opposite the window and he can look onto the distant hills and let his thoughts roam freely. There must, of course, be a climate of professionalism but this should be conveyed solely through the counsellor's bearing and personality.'

'So the first stage in the actual counselling process — after the counsellor's preparation — is that the person comes and is encouraged to speak freely.'

'The very first thing perhaps is that he feels he is not coming into a professional set-up because he would rather avoid that and is probably even scared of it; but that he feels he comes into an environment which is intimate, personal, and basically free of all clinical trappings. He should experience the counsellor as an ordinary, reasonably nice, and friendly human being. Then we settle down around the fire, not with a writing desk but only a little table between us. In order to help a new client to get accustomed to the surroundings, I ask him for his name, address and date of birth, and we have a few words about some general topic. There are two types of people. There are, firstly, those who are poised to unburden themselves right away; and they are, of course, encouraged to speak, and I listen. Then there are those who are very reluctant to speak and very often want me to ask them a few questions about their general background and education, and then they get going. Much of their problem is already expressed in this general account of their background.'

'The person who is very reluctant to speak or hardly comes out with any information, you will then really have to ask?'

'Yes, I give him plenty of time. Some people are very reluctant to come to the point and take a very long time to cover certain areas of their life before they disclose their problems. It's a matter of playing it by ear, and if I make a false move prematurely, that is to say if I intervene by focussing on the real problem area, which by that time I may have guessed already, he may take fright, withdraw and never come again. But if he goes on meandering and doesn't ever come to the point, then with careful timing, I ask him a leading question. But there are people who will avoid approaching a problem area even for weeks, while they cover and discuss the surrounding areas with reasonable competence, and there are cases where you must accept that, as long as you feel that the whole process of the encounter is fruitful and that the client is progressing. But there is one thing I always try to be quite certain about, and this is that the client comes of his own free will — that he is not being pushed or persuaded by friends, relations, a husband or a wife, etc, because counselling really presupposes *the conscious will of the client to co-operate.* He cannot be persuaded to co-operate, he cannot be coerced into co-operation; it is not the counsellor's business to involve him in the counselling process with some tricks of the trade. Therefore one of my first questions, if in doubt is, "Was it your own wish to come?" '

'We could perhaps come back to this when we talk about the kind of clients you would accept or refuse; it is an important point. Why do you think *listening* is so important and what actually happens to the listener? Obviously, it will give you all the information about the history of the person, about his feelings and problems. Apart from that, what happens to the client during this listening phase?'

'Well', responded Dr. Gregory, 'I think, in the first place, the client must experience that there is a person who is not only willing but keen to listen, to get to know him and to share his most intimate thoughts, feelings and experiences. That encourages him to speak out and to unburden himself. He will speak about things he probably has never spoken about before and that in itself is very therapeutic. But it is more than that. As he begins to articulate, to express these thoughts and feelings which so far have been held in, they suddenly "see the light of day", as we say. They are expressed and embodied in words, which now stand there, so to speak, in the space between the counsellor and the client; and if the client goes on articulating, he is for the first time face to face with his experiences, rather than being oppressed by them from within.'

'It occurs to me, as I listen to you, that one reason why people need counselling could be that in their own life, in their married life or within their circle of friends, they don't ever find the opportunity of expressing themselves, or they are never seen for what they really are.'

'No, that's it. In a crisis situation, I always discourage confiding in friends, relatives, etc. Quite frankly, I have hardly ever found that it will do much good. There are of course exceptional friends to whom a person can turn and unburden himself completely, but, as a rule, the relationship is too close, and people have their own ideas about the other person and about whatever the other person should do, so that they cannot accept him exactly as he is, without even inwardly putting any thoughts and ideas in the way.'

'Do you think any person close to the client would be too subjective perhaps and expect something of the client, whereas the counsellor has an objective relationship?'

'Yes. The counsellor has an objective relationship, and he doesn't expect anything; he doesn't hope for anything. You see, he waits for the moment when he can guide the client quite objectively into the next step of creative living. I give you an example from a quite different sphere which I think is illuminating. You know that I deal a lot with children. Now children very often need coaching, and two parties are specially concerned, namely, the teacher and the parents. Again, I have never seen any good coming from either teacher or parent undertaking the coaching because the relationship is too close. The teacher, as well as the parent, already expects some results from the child; he hopes for something and the child feels under pressure to produce something, which it is difficult for him to produce. That situation is too close and therefore it needs a third person who comes in from outside. The child will then feel free from demands of this kind; everything is objective, and in this atmosphere of freedom and with gentle encouragement, he will do what he is able to do, and very often he will blossom.'

'It occurs to me that in a marriage relationship one partner would always be giving advice or hoping for results from which he or she can benefit. I think this is only human, isn't it?'

'Yes. Discussions of marriage relationships between partners are most complex and stressful because the situation is heavily overlaid emotionally, and the expectations, hopes, tensions and frustrations are so strong. They are, therefore, very rarely fruitful.'

'Could we at this point summarise what the listening means to the client and what it means to the counsellor, Martin?'

'Well, the client in the first instance needs the relief of being completely himself, of being able fully to confide without reservation and to unburden himself without any inhibitions, without fearing to hurt anybody's feelings or "say something wrong". That in itself is a tremendous relief. The second benefit, I think, for the client is that as he articulates his thoughts and feelings, he becomes detached from them; for the first time he sees them as it were from a certain distance, because they have become embodied in words and they are no longer confined to his inner being. But, thirdly, I think that if the counsellor listens in the right way, following the client with complete selflessness as far as he is able, identifying with him, then, in a mysterious way, he reflects back onto the client not only what he expresses but also the client's own true being. I often compare it with a living mirror.'

'You are not talking now about interpreting what a client says?'

'Not at all', continued Dr. Gregory. 'I'm talking about relating to him in complete inner silence. And it may help you to understand what I mean here to share another of my favourite quotations. It is from Rudolf Steiner's book *Knowledge of the Higher Worlds*[2] and it comes in an early part of the book in the chapter called "The Stages of Initiation":

"...Of very great importance for the development of the student is the way in which he listens to others when they speak. He must accustom himself to do this in such a way that, while listening, his inner self is absolutely silent. If someone expresses an opinion, and another listens, assent or dissent will, generally speaking, stir in the inner self of the listener. Many people, in such cases, feel themselves impelled to an expression of their assent, or, more especially, of their dissent. In the student, all such assent or dissent must be silenced. It is not imperative that he should suddenly alter his way of living, by trying to attain at all times, this complete inner silence. He will have to begin by doing so in special cases, deliberately selected by himself. Then quite slowly and by degrees, this new way of listening will creep into his habits, as of itself. The student feels it is his duty to listen, by way of practice, at certain times, to the most contradictory views, and, at the same time, entirely to bring to silence all assent, and more especially, all adverse criticism. The point is, that, in so doing, not only all purely intellectual judgment be silenced, but also all feelings of displeasure, denial or even assent. The student must at all times be particularly watchful lest such feelings, even when not on the surface, should still lurk in the innermost recess of the soul...The student can thus train himself to listen to the words of others quite selflessly, completely shutting out his own person, and his opinions and way of feeling. When he practises listening without criticism, even when a completely contradictory opinion is advanced, when the most 'hopeless mistake' is committed before him, then he learns, little by little, to blend himself with the being of another and become identified with it. Then he hears through the words, into the soul of the other...."

And I'll give you one example of what I mean. The other day I had a young man here who is highly intelligent and who had thought about and searched through many spheres of philosophy, occultism, psychology, magic, and so on. Now, much of what he said was very foreign to me, and personally I couldn't agree with it all, for example when he said that Christ is the God of death, for to me Christ is the God of life. But I felt very strongly that I had to keep completely silent — not only outwardly but inwardly silent — and go with him along his rather tortuous pathways of experience and thought without deserting him. After he had related to me very extensively for about an hour and a half, without me interrupting him, the whole panorama and complexity of his experience, which he himself called weird — and weird it was! — and I was wondering how he would ever find a way out of this maze of thought and illusions, he suddenly said "But, you know, now I am through it all, now I have found the way back to myself, to my true humanity, and now I feel I can find my own God". I do think that, of course, he was prepared for this, but I do also think that I was somehow in the role of obstetrician, helping him to do this, to take the final step, simply by silently being with him and mirroring back to him not only what he said to me, namely, the weirdness of his experience, but also something different which was objective, which was not yet him, *something he wanted to become.* Hence I call it a living mirror, a mirror that responds quite silently, mirroring back something of the fundamental nature of man quite unconsciously. And this is perceived by the person who talks and in an almost telepathic way he may respond.'

'Could we come back to all that later on? At this point, do you ever make an assessment of the person's situation?'

'Yes, very much so. I use the word assessment only when I have to give a report to someone. For myself, I call this period of listening to the client a period of *exploration and identification;* it helps me to explore him and his world, in the same way that I should explore a city, by wandering about in it and getting to know exactly what it feels like, how it looks. Now, when I have completed this process, there are two things which I do: the first is what I call the *diagnostic interlude,* where I simply ask myself a clinical question about the health of the client, namely: Is he sufficiently healthy for me to be able to expect a rational response and co-operation from him? For instance, if he is seriously ill physically, say with a very painful duodenal ulcer, I can't expect this. Similarly, if he is, for example, suffering from a severe form of phobia, I can't expect it; and then I have to refer him, at least temporarily, to someone else. If, on the other hand, I feel that, although he has a certain disability, he will co-operate and can function on a rational level, I carry on.'

'Will you also assess his problem at this point? Would you say to yourself: "Now that I have entered into the life of this person, to what conclusions do I come?" '

'Yes, and this is now the next stage. After having disposed of the diagnostic issue, which is a clinical, intellectual problem, I try now to find, through living with him in his world, through this process of identification, the answer to the questions: In what way can I help him? What is missing in his life? What needs to be reshaped in his life? That may be something totally different from the problem he presented at the beginning. The young man I referred to a moment ago came with the problem that he was very shy; and so he was. He also had many intellectual and philosophical problems, as I have indicated. Now, the obvious answer would have been to help him through frequent conversations to overcome his shyness and to discuss or resolve his problems as far as possible. But after having lived inwardly with him in his world for a time — and, I emphasise, I *lived* rather than *thought* about it — I felt strongly that his relationship to life, his link with life, particularly with practical work, was not established, and I felt that the most essential thing for him to do was to take up physical work. This process of *assimilation* defies intellectual solutions; you can think about a person's predicament, but such mere thinking will not, anyway in my case, yield any reliable results, any results where I feel "That's it". It is the old rule of sleeping on it, it's a matter of handing over a question to the deeper layers of your being, to the unconscious, which is infinitely wiser than your head. And here again I'd like to quote Rudolf Steiner. The particular passage I have in mind comes from another of his works, *Practical Training in Thought*,[3] and occurs in the part of the book in which he insists on the importance of the ability to form and retain "exact pictures" of what is presented and therefore the details of scenes and impressions. Then he goes on to say in particular:

"...we must have the confidence that these events which in the outer world are connected with one another will also

13

bring about connections within us. This must be done in pictures only, *while abstaining from thinking*. One must say to oneself: 'I do not yet know what the relation is; but I shall let these things grow within me and they will bring about something in me if I refrain from speculation.' You will easily believe that if anyone forms exact inner images of succeeding events, at the same time *abstaining from all thinking*, something may be taking place in the invisible members of his nature".

Or, as I should put it myself, it is so important to develop the art of visualising in feeling-soaked images. If you have lived with questions and if you have learned patiently to let them mature in the depths of your being, then solutions and answers will come from deep within, with a sense of certainty and conviction. That, of course, takes time.'

'Does a client himself ever point to the real problem in the course of the counselling sessions?'

'The other day a young man came to see me who had a study problem. He had anxieties over his studies. He was a brilliant, gifted young man, and the obvious problem was to help him to get back to his studies and master his anxiety; but in the course of the session I felt that this wasn't the right course and I said to him: "Allow yourself to dream, and if you could have your way, quite apart from the practical possibilities, what would you like to do, how would you like to shape your life?" And he said: "I should like to live in the country, in a farmhouse with other people, near a river, work on the land; or I should like to go to Russia." He was a divinity student. And when he said this, I had to tell him: "This is exactly what I think, that is exactly what you need. That's the answer".

'Do you mean he was removed from the source of his strength?'

'Exactly. He was getting tired because he had been pressed very prematurely, as an eighteen year old, into the life of prayer and withdrawal of a Jesuit trainee, and that deprivation was the real problem, not the study. Therefore, if a person is sufficiently clear-headed, and courageous, he may sooner or later produce a solution, or something which indicates a solution and his real need, without me prompting, because deep down people feel what is lacking in their humanity, in their experience.'

'Could it possibly be the case that through expressing the problems, a sort of loosening up happens that makes it possible for a person to come up with the real issues?'

'Absolutely true, yes. I am sure it is a loosening up. As the conscious mind is relieved, the unconscious mind, which of course contains these images of hopes and expectations which are unfulfilled, has the possibility of coming to life and therefore will produce that. Moreover, if the counsellor is able to mirror back something like the totality of life, the totality of being human and of living, this will call out in the client a feeling of what he is lacking, and one way or another, he will indicate it; or even if he does not indicate it, he will, in most cases, respond to a suggestion — unless he is frightened, or simply unwilling to undertake the great effort and adventure of creative living. For it does need great courage, it needs effort and it needs truthfulness, and very many people are nowadays too far gone; they haven't got the courage any more, they haven't got the strength, they cannot rid themselves of old habits; and then very often they will tell me: "Yes, I know you're right; but I'm sorry, I can't do it", and they vanish.'

'Can we look again over the different stages of counselling process we have covered so far, then?' asked Bridget.

'Yes. I think we have discussed and to some extent characterised *four* distinct stages of the counselling process so far, namely, the *preparation,* which concerns the counsellor only, but is fundamental to the counselling process; secondly, the process of *listening,* or, as we have also called it, the stage of exploration and identification; then, number three, the *diagnostic interlude;* and number four — and I think that this is a distinct phase — the time which the counsellor requires in order fully to *assimilate* into his unconscious mind the totality of the client's being and situation, where he hands over, so to speak, the questions in his mind to the deeper layers of his being and waits for the answer to come; because he has far greater wisdom than he himself has intellectually at his disposal. So, in this sense, I think we have covered four distinct phases: 1. preparation; 2. listening, exploration and identification; 3. diagnostic interlude; 4. assimilation, (and 3 and 4 are interchangeable).'

'The assimilation will eventually culminate in some clear understanding of the person's needs, or the person's problems? But you don't think it out. My impression, from the way you put it, is that you live with the problem and the answer comes up, wells up, from the deeper layers within you?'

'Yes. I have always experienced that when I try to think and think, I become rather more uncertain than certain, while, if I allow myself this time of living with it, of assimilation into the deeper layers of the mind, eventually I reach a point where I feel completely certain. I have a private expression for this, namely, that "something hits me under the belt"; I feel from deep within that I'm being almost physically gripped, I feel "That's it". I was interested to come across a Japanese proverb which at the moment I can't recall in detail but which expresses exactly this: this feeling of arriving at certainty through an unconscious process, which hits you, so to speak, below the diaphragm.'

'So it's really quite a vital process?'

'I believe that in the whole counselling process this is perhaps the most vital. We must not under-estimate how vital, how subtle, preparation is, how subtle exploration is; even the diagnostic interlude requires subtle decision-making; but the most personal phase of the counselling process, which requires the greatest patience and the confidence that life itself will give you the answer, that the very being of the client will give you the answer and not your intellectual reasoning — the most vital, the most subtle phase of the counselling, is what I call for want of a better word, "assimilation". It will enable the counsellor, out of the certainty which he now experiences, out of the clarity of the vision which will suddenly highlight for him certain areas that may have been indistinct or covered by a kind of shadow, to select what we may call a *target area* or several target areas. He can now make the decision to work on these; and that brings us to stage five.'

'So the process has really gone from the more unconscious layers of experience to a conscious level where you can actually turn it into concepts and select the area or the approach to the solution of the problems?'

'Precisely. It is then conceptualised, it is then made a target, it is pin-pointed; and at this point I do write down for myself, very briefly, what I call a *therapy programme,* essentially a number of *target-areas,* which I hope to be able to approach and work through with the client, as time goes on. That may take a few sessions, it may take months, that depends on the relationship as it develops and, of course, particularly on the personality and the response of the client'.

'How far do you discuss this therapy programme with the client? Is it something you have at the back of your mind? How far do you disclose to a client how you see his problem, how you see his situation?'

'I have it essentially at the back of my mind, in a very tentative form. If this were too firm a structure which I tried to impose and convey too strongly, too distinctly to the client, I should stifle the therapeutic process. The therapeutic process is something which must flow freely in terms of feeling, encounter and conversation between the client and the therapist. Therefore, when a session begins, although I do tentatively have at the back of my mind what I might discuss with the client, I try to feel how he is feeling, to tune in to it and give him ample opportunity to express what is foremost in his mind. This may, for example, be something which has just happened to him last week and which he has a very great need to tell me; and of course it would be a very great mistake to stop him. Or other thoughts may have occurred to him meantime. But if, as the session proceeds, I feel that his mind is more relaxed, I try to sense whether this is possibly the right moment to steer the conversation back towards the target area or towards a specific objective which I have in mind.'

'Does the client to some degree share this objective with you?'

'Ideally, of course, he should share it fully. This is perhaps too much to expect, but I think that it is essential that, at some point at least, *he has accepted it intellectually;* namely, that he will say to me: "I think that you're right, I can see the sense of what you say." If, for example, I say to this young man: "I think you should do physical labour", he will agree and say, "Yes, I think that's a good idea; this is what I really need". However, it may take a very long time for this to be translated into sufficiently strong feeling and particularly sufficiently strong initiative to become reality. Or, to give you another example: I had a young woman who was leading a very promiscuous life; she was, on the one hand, enjoying it because she felt confirmed as a woman; on the other hand, of course, quite inevitably she was extremely miserable about it and was unable to support a steady relationship. Now, I felt I should make it clear to her that her promiscuous life was having a destructive effect on her personality as well as on her ability to support a steady relationship and eventually enter a happy marriage; to which, intellectually, she fully agreed, she saw the point. Now, she was one of those unfortunate people whose ways of life and habits were so deeply ingrained that she could no longer do without it. This can be compared with an addiction. If you depend on a drug, you may not be able to wean yourself off it; similarly promiscuity can become an addiciton. So it was with her. In the end, it was she who said, "I know your're quite right, but I'm sorry, I can't do it", and she went for good. You see, there are limits to what a counsellor or any human being can do. You must always keep in mind that ultimately the decision is the client's, it is he who has to make up his mind.'

'You are working with a person's motivation, you are encouraging his growth; but the person has to do the growing himself?'

'Yes, towards what I call creative living. And creative living is living which leads a person to a greater capacity to overcome difficulties and so to learning very gradually and painfully to achieve mastery over himself and his circumstances. This is how Goethe describes it in *Wilhelm Meister's Apprenticeship:*

"Probably the greatest thing that can be said to a man's credit is that he succeeds in determining circumstances to the greatest extent possible and to the least extent is subject to their determination. The whole world lies before us like a great quarry before the architect. But only he deserves this name who succeeds in using these natural blocks to give substance to an archetypal intuition with the greatest economy, purposiveness and solidity. Everything outside is only material (and I would include even the outer layer of the self in this term); but deep down in the core there is this creative power, the capacity to create what is to be, and the urge to tolerate no let down until we have given it shape in one way or another, either outside ourselves or in our own person". (Quoted in *Goethe: Wisdom and Experience,* at p.164).

This struggle will lead him sooner or later within the limits of his possibilities towards a truer and more complete humanity. The woman we have been discussing is miserable, she feels that life is defeating her, or rather that she has treated life the wrong way. She is, as every human being is, motivated towards growing, towards overcoming difficulties, towards turning defeat into victory, but the motivation was not strong enough, and as I said before, her strength failed her. It is a matter of strength, it is a matter of effort.'

'Could we for a moment talk about the aims and objectives of counselling, Martin? Am I right in thinking that what you have just voiced are really the aims and objectives as you see them? Would you consider the growing towards creative living as the aim? Could you enlarge on that a bit?'

'I think that this is the ideal or overall aim', continued Dr. Gregory. 'We might say that the aims of counselling are twofold. The first aim is to enable the client to gain a vision of life in its completeness, in its fullness, in its reality. You have probably come across a rather famous saying of Matthew Arnold: "To see life steadily and to see it whole" (referring to Sophocles). I find this an admirable formula to describe what we all need: a vision to see life steadily and to see it whole. This is something which I try consciously or subconsciously to convey to the client, if only to a limited extent. His job then, and our job as human beings, is to adjust to this wholeness of life, to become steady, to unfold, and to develop in such a way that we become, as far as possible, complete human beings, rather than problem-burdened fragments. Or, to put it in other words, our general aim is to become more and more of a piece with this totality and not with just part of it, to become adjusted emotionally, intellectually and spiritually. That is, of course, the ideal blueprint, and you can achieve this only in part, if you can achieve it at all. But what you might be able to achieve, and I see this as the second aim of counselling, is the establishment of *growing-points*. You will not discharge a client as a complete human being fully adjusted to the totality of life; but you will have given him an impetus to grow, you will have given him motivation, perhaps the courage to overcome difficulties, to change himself, to adapt to life in a new way; and that will be the beginning of a long process, which he will continue without you. And to achieve even this you may well have to help him to attain some more immediate and concrete objective.'

'You do not measure the way a person has gone. You are thinking in terms of sowing seeds from which future developments can happen?'

'This is largely what I do. For example, I do not think that the case of the promiscuous young woman is hopeless. She has experienced and accepted a different view of life; only at this point in her life, she was unable to make it a practical issue, she didn't have the strength. She will probably go through a great deal of suffering, and it is possible that the suffering will in the end bring her to a point where she will find new resources and strength so far undiscovered. But of course I should not be content with establishing only growing-points; I want to establish and achieve practical results. For example, coming back to the young man who should do physical labour, I want to bring him to the point where he goes to the labour exchange and gets a job; and not only that, but to the point where he gets a job and maintains it, which is a lot more. This bring us to two further stages of the counselling process. I believe it was stage five when we opened out the target areas. Now the next stage is that we focus the client more and more directly on the *goal, on the future*. Whereas, when he came, he experienced his life fundamentally as the life which he had lived, the experience of the past, and very often the great difficulties and the stagnation of the present; now as the result of work in the target area he should become future orientated; because, in my view, man is a being made to reach out towards the future. This is what he really wants: to go forward, to live and grow or, as St Paul says, "forgetting what lies behind and straining forward to what lies ahead". This is a monumental saying, of a tremendous man with a great mission, and we must not make the mistake of applying it to us very ordinary mortals, because we cannot all simply forget what lies behind. But essentially we can leave it behind and we should try to do better. I then hope to reach the point where I can enable the client to be more and more conscious of what lies ahead for him in various spheres of life: practical work, relationships, inner development and so on; so that the shadows of the past and the difficulties of the present become comparatively negligible, and the vision of the future lies open; that, I believe is stage six. Stage seven supervenes when he actually *steps into his future*, makes a new life, re-shapes his outer and inner existence; in the case of the young man, when he begins to do physical work, finds new relationships and, of course, correspondingly has a new outlook and a different attitude. Now, in this process, and in this great adventure of creative living, again I feel I have to support him, because he may encounter many pitfalls, setbacks, difficulties and so on, whether it is work, or whether it is entering into a new relationship such as an engagement period or marriage. These, I think, are the seven stages', said Dr. Gregory.

'Well, that is really a lot to take in. It is a wonderfully hopeful outlook on the abilities of human beings.'

'I think that the counsellor, however pessimistic he may be about the present situation in our society must have a fundamental faith in man. I have got that through my encounters with people; they have aroused in me, in spite of difficulties and disappointments, the utmost admiration for their resourcefulness, their resilience. I find their honesty and truthfulness absolutely staggering; and whenever I encounter people who reveal themselves in utter honesty and truthfulness to me, I feel ashamed of the sham and lie which is lived in our conventional society. The situation of the counsellor and the client is, of course, taken completely out of the context of ordinary social life: it is an encounter on a remote island, there are only these two people there and the sky above them, and then human nature reveals itself. It has brought out in me, as I said, the utmost admiration for the strength and the truthfulness of people and their will to go forward in life. Then the spirituality which is now awakening in people, their need to understand, as far as they can see, this mysterious universe and to unite with it as far as possible, has made me feel thoroughly humble. And I have at times felt very, very common and very ordinary, confronted with some of the young people whom I call the rare spirits. There are tremendous things going on in human beings and I think the counsellor is in a very privileged position to recognise that, whilst he also simultaneously has to recognise the appalling decline which takes place in the nature of a person who allows himself to drift and is not making the tremendous effort of creative living, reshaping his own personality, his own destiny, his own life. As the people who do that go forward to the distant goal of humankind, the others go down and deteriorate into lying, into brutality, into disorganised ways of life. Here we reach the parting of the ways, and the counsellor's business is to help those along who try to find the way forward, who are truly future orientated.'

'Do you think I have really grasped what you said when I summarise the aims of counselling as being a matter of helping a person to develop his potential?'

'Yes, to the fullest possible extent, to develop his humanity. Of course, the human personality is fragmentary and limited; but there are always untapped resources in all of us; and I think it becomes more and more important that people, instead of becoming high-powered specialists in some fields, with a tremendous income and with a highly specialised skill and knowledge, become true persons, true human beings, who are capable of living; because living is a very great art and it has to be learned. There was even a book called *Teach Yourself to Live*. We are a very long way from really grasping that the art of living presupposes the art and the effort of becoming human and remaining human, which is again another issue. The people who neglect their humanity for the sake, for example, of their professional or intellectual progress or their money-earning capacity, almost invariably founder in life. I have met some brilliant university professors, very nice people, but totally incapable of living, totally incapable of maintaining a reasonable relationship with their wives, or solving the simplest human problem. One of the fundamental faculties which I believe is to a large extent lost now and which only a true person and a reasonably complete person can recover is judgment. That sounds very simple; but judgment is in my view and in my experience a very rare commodity, because it is made, in a curious way, out of a fusion of feeling, intuition, and reasoning; and only a person who is reasonably complete will be able to achieve that. A man may be extremely clever in his own field, brilliantly clever; but as far as life is concerned, he may have no judgment at all.'

'Nowadays', said Bridget, 'we are called to rely more and more upon our own judgment because standards are disintegrating. The possibilities are endless; everything is changing, and we constantly have to make judgments out of our own capacity; we cannot fall back on saying: "This is the way it is done." '

'Yes, there are more and more courses about the way in which certain things have to be done. You are taught how to talk, you are taught how to communicate, you can take a course on shaping relationships, you can take a course on decision-making. In the end, you will have to take a course on which foot you should put first. I mean, life becomes more and more complicated and people inevitably become increasingly uncertain and confused. You see, in my view, much of this could be avoided if, instead of intellectually analysing these various spheres of existence, we concentrated our energies on becoming true human beings.'

'So your aim, Martin, is for a person to become a true human being, as far as it is individually possible?'

'Yes, that again may sound easy, but it is really extremely difficult and it requires courage, truthfulness and a merciless recognition of your own weaknesses. Also appreciation of your assets and the will to develop them. In order to become a true person you have to renounce certain pleasures, forego certain liberties you would like to take but shouldn't. To give you a simple example again: you simply cannot allow yourself to be involved in too much talking or gossiping, attending too many lectures or conferences and social events. There are limits. You must have periods of silence, in order to collect yourself as a human being. You have to practise restraint, control, whether it concerns food or drink, travel, exercise or relationships. Time and again you will have to weigh your inner stillness, your poise and serenity against the impact of these various active ties. You will have to establish a strict personal discipline, as it were a rule of life, self-created and self-imposed. Naturally this requires your readiness to make sacrifices, which may cause you discomfort or may even be painful. But the result will justify the sacrifice. Rufolf Steiner once said that "creative sacrifice" (*schöpferische Verzicht*) achieved and sustained in stillness opens up undreamt of sources of spiritual strength'.

Notes

1. Jolande Jacobi *Jung, Psychological Reflections* (Pantheon Books Inc. New York, 1953 at p.71).

2. Rudolf Steiner *Knowledge of the Higher Worlds and its Attainment* (Anthroposophic Press Inc. New York, 1947 at pp.32-33).

3. Rudolf Steiner *Practical Training in Thought* (Anthroposophic Press Inc. New York, 1948 p.13).

dialogue 2: counselling and the archetype of the human dialogue

'I was extremely interested to read the transcript of the conversation you had with your friend, Bridget, the social worker', I began this morning's conversation by saying. 'This particular series of dialogues between us began when I asked you some time ago what was involved in psychotherapy. You then said, if I may sum up your reply, that four things were required: an all-round knowledge of man arising from the widest possible experience of people, life, art and religion; the possession on the part of the counsellor of a personality formed by a deliberate spiritual training; a basic attitude, that of one human being as a whole meeting another human being as a whole in a spirit of highly-disciplined listening and respect; and a basic skill in dealing with people. You then went on to deal principally with this last aspect, explaining how a counselling relationship would typically unfold in seven stages, in much the same way as you had already done, unbeknown to me, with Bridget. And what I now see, after having been able to read the transcript of your conversation with her, is that you were able to give me such a clear and profound account not only because you had already responded to a similar request from Bridget but because before this you had spent years — over twenty years — exploring and practising all this intuitively in your work as a paediatrician and counsellor with children and adults. In other words, your practice came well before your reflection.'

'Yes', Dr. Gregory replied. 'These seven stages simply emerged in the discussion with Bridget. As I talked with her, I began to realise that there is a certain organic sequence of stages. As our conversation proceeded, I discovered that I do instinctively go from one to the next and that a certain process, a dynamism, is there, and this dynamic can then be sub-divided into these seven stages: preparation; listening and exploration; the diagnostic interlude; assimilation; the selection of a target area or areas; helping the client to focus on the future; supporting the client as he steps out into this future. I was rather surprised by this at first, and then I was encouraged by discovering that David Stafford-Clark had also described a dynamic principle underlying the therapeutic encounter, albeit in a different way. In his view, if you recall, insight therapy, as he calls it in *Psychiatry for Students*[1] develops in three essential phases: Receiving, Assimilating, Intervening. Therefore I did not start with Stafford-Clark, but I was subsequently glad to find that his was an independent variant of the method I have gradually evolved.'

'And it is this seven-stage dynamic that you have since reproduced for me, with this difference, that when you did so, you added various refinements of what you had previously said to Bridget. And the chief refinement, as I understand it, was that the concept of preparation for any individual counselling session was much richer. On the one hand, by the time you expressed your reflection on your practice to me, you had come to see more clearly that the preparation — your stage one — was really the preparation of the whole personality of the counsellor, in particular through a sustained spiritual discipline. Strictly speaking, therefore, one should think of the spiritual training of the counsellor not as something lying as it were alongside or parallel to the practice of counselling in its seven stages but as something penetrating the very substance of the counsellor's personality or activity. But, it seems to me, this has so many implications that I should like to discuss it with you on another occasion.'

'I should be delighted to do so', Dr. Gregory replied. 'But may I say in the meantime that when I first spoke with you about the whole complex of factors involved in psychotherapy, I did indeed distinguish, on the one hand, the basic attitude of listening, which is crucial in the process of counselling, and, on the other hand, the humanity as well as the spirituality of the counsellor, whereas now I should stress how all these elements interpenetrate each other. The spiritual training is not simply a specific training in spiritual skills and achievements but presupposes the counsellor's total humanity. It is this that must form the basis of his spiritual development, otherwise he would become a sort of dehydrated saint, which is a lamentable condition. And in this connection, we thought of the great examples of St. Augustine and St. Francis of Assisi who first lived fully human lives and then transmuted and refined them into spiritual energy and experience. In modern times we have the example of Thomas Merton who was also very much a man of the world before he submitted himself to the monastic cell.'

'There are many others', I added, 'for example, Charles de Foucauld, Martin Luther King and Dorothy Day who died only recently.'

'And, of course, one of the greatest examples, if not the greatest of all, is the Buddha.'

'So all that is a big subject, Martin, and I very much look forward to exploring it with you another day. To return, however, to the other aspect of the refinement of what you had said to Bridget in your subsequent re-exploration of the subject with me, you insisted that the most important single factor in counselling is the personality of the counsellor, so that the real preparation for any particular counselling session is the whole life that the counsellor brings to any such session.'

'Yes', said Dr. Gregory, 'and it is perhaps here that I have really moved on in my thinking since I last spoke on this subject even with you. The seven stages which I explained to Bridget and then again to you represent the way I have gradually come to articulate what I should like to call the dynamic of a therapeutic encounter. But what has become clear to me only recently is that this seven-stage dynamic is basic *not only* to the therapeutic encounter *but also* to the human encounter as this manifests itself in the *Gespräch*. And by *Gespräch* I denote any meaningful conversation, a truly human dialogue, where people raise fundamental questions, exchange basic impressions, and where they both grope for some kind of direction, for some kind of, if not ultimate solution, at least some provisionally valid approach to these questions. And I think that if you scrutinise these seven stages, you will see that they also apply, though perhaps in a slightly modified way, to the process and dynamism, the organic dynamism, of an ordinary *Gespräch*, provided only that this is meaningful.

And that seems to me to be quite important. For example, I have discovered that when I am due to have a *Gespräch* with a friend, I have to go into this kind of preparatory stage of silence and recollection, exactly as I do with a client. To take another example: You may say, "Well, what about the diagnostic interlude? Surely you don't make a diagnosis when you meet one of your friends?" No, of course I don't make a diagnosis. But you see, in order to be sensitive to the needs of a person, you have to assess — in inverted commas –"diagnostically" what kind of condition this person is in, what you can say to him, what will be helpful or significant, how much he can take, and so on. You see, in this sense, a kind of "diagnosis", something comparable to a diagnosis, will come into it.

So we have here something quite fundamental, and I think it is fundamental in the sense that, as I now see things, the seven-stage process works not only in the therapeutic encounter but in the truly human encounter, the *Gespräch* as such. And in this respect it is different from Stafford-Clark's scheme since he applies it only to the therapeutic encounter. Then I should like to make one more point. But is that alright so far?'

'Yes, yes. I understand very well', I replied. 'It is as if your practice of counselling had come long before your reflection on it, but also as if, once you had begun to reflect on this practice with Bridget and then with me, the dynamic of your practice had continued, but now in a different mode. The same dynamic which eventually prolonged your practice into reflection has now been at work in the process of reflection itself, so that what began as an articulation of the practice of the *counselling relationship* has worked even freer to become the articulation of *any* true and deep human relationship, as manifested in the *Gespräch*. What you have recently come to, then, is a deepening and a widening of the significance of the sevenfold dynamic?'

'Precisely', said Dr. Gregory. 'It now has a wider social significance. It is as such that it has a profoundly human significance. You see, once you have absorbed these attitudes and allowed them to become instinctive, then, whenever you have a human encounter, you will somehow go through these seven stages of preparation, exploration, assimilation, and so forth. There is, however, a difficult question here. I have been asked: "If that is so, how do the various therapies come in? I mean, what about Freud, what about Jung, what about behaviour therapy, and so on?" This is a very important question. If the sevenfold process has a basically human significance, where do particular therapeutic methods, as distinct from the general therapeutic encounter, come in?

Now, I think the answer, as far as I can see, is this: you remember that we spoke of a target area which has to be selected (our stage 5). And then we said that we have to work through this target area (our stage 6). Now I think that it is here, when we have selected a target area, that we have to make up our mind what therapeutic method, if any, we are to use. Right? For example, if you have a person who has a neurosis, a claustrophobia, and he can't go out or be in a closed room, you've got to do something about this, and after you have cleared other target areas you want to concentrate on this. The question then is: how do you do it? You see, you can decide on an analytical method, or you can decide on dream interpretation, or on suggestion, or simply on the "talking" therapy. You can also decide on conditioning therapy. You can, for instance, say that for this particular person, it is best to take him out in a car with you. *In this way, I think, specific therapeutic methods or techniques can be inserted into the complete process at this juncture and are built into the whole structure of the human encounter. Therefore the structure as such, I think, remains unchanged and is, as it were, archetypal.'*

'That is very interesting. Because that answers a question I have been very much considering within myself. You see, I have some acquaintance with some methods. But more and more I'm convinced of their relativity and therefore of the need to adjust and to choose the exact method for each person. I have been dealing with three people recently to whom I instinctively just listened as totally as possible, and, without having conceptualised it in the way you have, I think I came to something like a diagnostic interlude, when I asked myself: what does this particular person need? And it does seem to vary, so that to use one method only is to put people in a procrustean bed.'

'Absolutely', said Dr. Gregory with enthusiasm. 'You see, the upshot of it all is that what I am talking about is not a specific therapeutic method, just one more added to the great number that already exist. No, these stages express the archetypal pattern of the therapeutic and human encounter as such, and this is basic and therefore unalterable. And into this has to be built, and can be built, any, but any, therapeutic method or technique. *Therefore this type of counselling or Gesprächstherapie has no quarrel with any other psychological or analytic method. It recognises all of them as far as they are valid and free of error. So it is also capable of and open to using them, but with discrimination, and it is not committed to any one specifically.* And as you indicated, the methods of therapy can be as unlimited as the possibilities of life itself. But the therapy must be specificially selected. You see, any human activity and human experience can ultimately, if rightly placed, work as a therapy. At the same time, they each have their limitations, and so can complement each other. I do, however, believe that the most fundamental and ultimately most powerful therapy is the therapy of the human encounter as such, where the very being of the therapist heals. Of course, we're at the very beginning of experiences of this kind, and of such possibilities. I think that it would, therefore, be a fatal mistake in the training of therapists and psychiatrists to underestimate the importance of the maturity and the spirituality of the personality which is then conveyed to the client, and to concentrate the training only on the technicalities of a method or of a school of thought or the clinical aspect, whatever it may be.

May I take it still a stage further? You see, more and more people who have all sorts of spiritual experiences, whether through meditation or spontaneously, are now coming in touch not only with priests but with analysts and psychiatrists. And psychiatrists who are ignorant of the spiritual dimension of human nature and the kind of spiritual experience people are capable of having react to them — and I have two particular cases in mind — as if such people were simply suffering from aberrations. And this just won't work. Because events of this kind will simply explode into our, in this respect, complacent society. It just won't work for a psychiatrist to say, "Oh, well, this is a depressed and deluded person" because they are very often not depressed or half-mad. All the more important therefore that we deepen our experience in this human and spiritual realm in order to be able to face what is coming.'

'This explosion of the spiritual?', I asked.

'Yes. But that's only by the way. It's at a tangent to what we were discussing, namely, the relationship of this basic human encounter as embodied in these stages to specific therapeutic techniques, whether psychiatric, analytic or other techniques or methods of healing, from the crudely physical to the spiritual — the whole range.'

'That may indeed be something of a digression, Martin', I said, 'but it does follow on from what you were saying about the inner development of your thinking on the subject of the deeper significance of the process of the therapeutic encounter. To return, however, to the main point, I find this latter notion fascinating; and at the deepest level I am captivated by it. At another level, however, I feel certain difficulties about this latest stage of your thinking. But before I attempt to express these difficulties to you, may I recapitulate what we have discussed so far? When I asked you in what proved to be the first in this series of discussion what was involved in psychotherapy, you said that in your opinion there are four main things: first, the widest possible experience of life and people; secondly, a sustained spiritual discipline; thirdly, a basic attitude of one human being seeking to listen to and respond to another human being; and, fourthly, a developed skill in gradually eliciting the other's potential for growth and managing his own destiny. It was primarily with this latter skill that you dealt in your discussion with Bridget, whereas it was with the general presuppositions that you dealt in your discussion with me. Now, with hindsight, I can see that there was, as I mentioned before, an inner dynamic to your own life, practice and thinking, so that your thinking seemed to be a continuation of your practice, and your latest thinking a continuation of both. I can further see that in the latest stage of your thinking, as you have expressed it to me today, you have penetrated the deepest meaning of the therapeutic encounter and thereby uncovered the *structure of any inter-personal communication,* into which any form of therapy can be fitted — the inner structure, therefore, as you put it, of the archetypal human encounter *tout court,* as this is then manifested in the *Gespräch.* This conclusion therefore seems to have the singular force of a certain inevitability; it is like some pure distillate — and not only of your own prolonged experience but of a far larger, more universally human experience of which your particular experience is therefore like an alembic. For all that, however, with my analytic self I still have these nagging doubts. So what I should like to do now, Martin, partly for the sake of the clarification of the ideas in my own mind and partly for the sake of truth and completeness, is to go over the seven stages and to check whether we can in fact transpose the description of the encounter between counsellor and client into a description of the encounter between one human being and another. For, if your thesis is valid, we can now analyse the truly human encounter in the same terms, so that every stage of the therapeutic encounter should correspond one by one, in its own way, with an ordinary but deep conversation — such, for instance, as the one we're having now. For presumably this discussion obeys the same law, to the extent that it is a true *Gespräch*?'

'Yes, indeed', Dr. Gregory agreed.

'Well', I continued, 'the first stage — if I make a mistake, you'll correct me, won't you? — is that a client tries to explain himself, and you made a distinction between the presenting and the real problem.'

'No, not quite', Dr. Gregory interrupted. 'The first stage is really the stage of preparation. Now this applies to the visit of a friend as well as to a session with a client. So here I visualise somebody coming who I know will want to discuss something of personal importance. Quite briefly, I withdraw into this room about ten or fifteen minutes before. Then the friend or the client arrives, and, assuming I know him, I try to keep perfectly still. I quiet my mind so that I know I shall be quite receptive. I do not *think* about him but *visualise* him, so that I can get a feeling of the kind of world he lives in, the feeling of the atmosphere which is peculiarly his own. That is the preparation, right? And that applies to visiting friends as well as to clients. Then stage two is simply the stage of observing, listening, exploring, with the main emphasis on listening. Now the friend will tell me something about what he's coming for, what he wants to discuss. Apart from listening, I make myself open in exactly the same way as with a client, I try to explore his special situation at this moment in his life. That is to say, I'll ask certain questions in order to be able to get as rounded an impression as possible of his situation, his relationships, the kind of life he leads, for example.'

'You're talking about a *Gespräch* between friends now? Not a therapeutic encounter?', I asked.

'It's exactly the same', Dr. Gregory replied.

'So, presumably, between two people who are similarly minded, the reverse could happen? I mean, he could also explore you? To the extent that you're on the same wavelength, there might be reciprocity?'

'Yes, that's perfectly true', Dr. Gregory agreed.

'Isn't there, therefore, a certain assymetry between the situation of the counsellor and client and that of friend and friend? As between friends there's absolute equality, isn't there?', I asked.

'Strictly as between friend and friend, yes, I agree', answered Dr. Gregory, 'but perhaps I'm biased in a certain way. I must admit that it happens so rarely in my life — the process of reciprocity — that I'm conditioned...'

'Exactly, that's what I mean', I interjected. 'What I detect is that the model of counsellor and client is still so dominant in your life and therefore in your thinking that you haven't really worked the application of your insight right through to do justice to the relationship of two equals. And what I wonder is what happens when two people are really equal, whether it's two friends, as, say in our situation (I hope!), or as between husband and wife, where neither is playing the role of father or mother, if you like of superior, where they're wrestling equally with each other and with some common problem. Then perhaps the model breaks down to a certain extent, doesn't it?'

'I don't know, I'm not at all sure', said Dr. Gregory.

'But surely you do have to alter the model somewhat in this particular instance', I said, 'because the relationship of counsellor and client is really on the basis of, well, of superior and inferior, of one who has something to give and of another who has to ask, whereas in the case of true friends, it is a common search. There's a dependency in one case, which is absent in the other, isn't there?'

'Yes, but I think that "superior" and "inferior" are terms...', Dr. Gregory demurred.

'They're not good terms', I agreed.

'No, they're not terms I should be inclined to use', Dr. Gregory continued. 'But I think, as far as I can judge it now, that the answer to your question is not that the model breaks down, but that the two participants explore and function so to say simultaneously, according to the same basic pattern. For instance, they would have to listen to each other, observe each other in order really to understand and to get somewhere. The usual breakdown and the loss of meaning in conversation has its root in the fact that this very thing doesn't happen. Either the whole thing falls apart or it becomes one-sided.'

'Well, Martin, I'm very glad that you have now explicitly allowed for the element of reciprocity. The trouble is that, by doing so, you have made rather a difficulty for youself, as it seems to me. The problem arises as follows. The intuition you have recently come to is that the therapeutic encounter is only a variant of what you call the archetypal human encounter, and that an analysis of the therapeutic encounter is therefore substantially an analysis of the archetypal human encounter. But you have come to your sevenfold analysis through your experience of the therapeutic encounter. The question, therefore, is whether there is really an equivalent of each of your seven stages in a simply human *Gespräch* once one allows for the element of reciprocity which exists between equal friends and which does not exist between counsellor and client. In other words, can we restate your sevenfold analysis in such a way that it does justice to the mutality of an ordinary but true dialogue? So what we need to do now is to resume the attempt, but now systematically, to check that a *Gespräch* does indeed unfold through your seven phases as much as the therapeutic process does.'

'Yes, yes. You see, deep down, I'm convinced that it is so. I've not been challenged to articulate it so clearly before. But just let me try, and we'll see how far we get. So, again starting at the beginning: Stage one, I prepare myself, by sitting quietly, because I want to be ready for the *Gespräch,* and not be full of my own thoughts. Stage two: my friend comes. Now when the friend has come, I watch, listen, observe, and try to find out what his life-situation and his state of mind are, exactly as I do — of course, in a modified form — with a client. Now, as I said before, then we come to the diagnostic interlude, Stage three. Here again you might say, "The thing doesn't work". But I believe that in every basic human encounter you have to assess what your friend's mood is, what his general state of health is, whether he is tired or fresh, how much he can take, what you will say to him, how you will say it. In that sense it is a variant of the diagnostic interlude.'

'Except that we now have to add that it is reciprocal. Ideally the friend should do the same for you?', I interjected.

'Yes'

'There should be a mutual sensitivity, so that neither forces anything on the other beyond his capacity.'

'Yes. It's very interesting that it's you who make this point', Dr. Gregory said, 'because it usually happens in one direction in my case so that I'm hardly aware of this mutality — though I must say that my friends are very much aware whether I'm tired or not. So in this sense you're quite right, it's reciprocal. So then, we come to Stage four, the stage of assimilation. Of course in every *Gespräch*, as in every encounter with a client, this process can happen very rapidly. Ideally it is a process which should be allowed to proceed and mature slowly. I mean that, after you have gained an impression of the personality and of the world of relationships of this person, you should live with these images and assimilate them slowly. But very often conditions force you to act very quickly, and you select, or you are "hit" by, certain significant images or it may be only a gesture. And the same applies to the encounter with your friend. Here too you have to assimilate, usually very quickly, unless you feel you need time, in which case you should say so, if it is a very important talk. You assimilate, almost half consciously, a certain range of impressions and images which you feel are essential for this person, and to this you will respond.'

'I'm just thinking, Martin, that you seem in the very way you're describing things to have slipped back into talking from the point of view of a counsellor. And I'm always trying to visualise a situation where you're *both* clients, if you like, where you're both equal. So that the process is reciprocal, and then, it seems to me, it isn't just a question of one person entering into the feeling world and images of the other but of both entering into the feeling world of each other. And perhaps more than that, it's a question of trying to enter into and slowly construct a *common* world of feelings and images, isn't it? Because, as you said at the beginning, in any human *Gespräch*, you don't really know where you're going, you're groping for something together.'

'Yes, I agree. But the essential thing is that even if you put it like that, which I accept, it would still mean that what happens in the therapeutic encounter has a parallel in the meaningful and mutually helpful human encounter of the *Gespräch* where two people want to find each other with a feeling of gain in understanding, not only of each other but of themselves and of life.'

'Yes, I can accept that, Martin. Once again the assimilation that takes place is mutual. That's the major modification to make.'

'Yes, you've made me aware of a completely new dimension and aspect of the matter, which I wasn't aware of, namely, that the process can happen simultaneously in two directions. And then it's all the more valid and valuable. And quite clearly, if we take Stage six, the working through...'

'What about Stage five, the selection of the target area?' I interrupted. 'What's the equivalent of that in a *Gespräch*?'

'Well, it's the target area that is psychologically or practically the most essential thing in a *Gespräch*. In other words, you don't woffle, you don't drift. You have a directed, a purposeful conversation, you want to go somewhere, and that you can do only if you follow a certain direction.'

'Would you say it's a question of agreeing upon an issue?'

'Yes, exactly, it's a question of agreeing on an issue in the sense that either your friend or you yourself move towards an issue, and then you both feel that it's the right one. And if you feel, as you move in a certain direction, that you're going in the wrong direction, you redirect yourself. So much for the target area. Then you begin to work through that in order to arrive at a conclusion that will give you some reassurance or comfort or a feeling of fresh vitality. This would be Stage six. And, finally, you see, Stage seven, guiding the client into a new pattern of life, translated into terms of a purely human *Gespräch*, becomes the feeling which we sum up by saying at the conclusion of a conversation with a friend, "That was a good talk". What do we mean by that? We mean either that we go out into life and know better how to handle certain situations, how to think about certain problems, or, even if this doesn't apply, we go back refreshed, with a new zest for life, and with a sense that we have left behind the trivialities, concentrated on something worthwhile and therefore have gained in vitality.'

'Yes, I can see that, Martin. Now it seems to me that two things have emerged from our attempt to translate the analysis of the therapeutic encounter between counsellor and client into an analysis of basic human dialogue. First, I think that you and I have

35

both seen more clearly that we have to be very aware of the difference between the two situations, and therefore have to modify the description of the *Gespräch* to take account of the vital element of reciprocity which I think you're always inclined *not* to do. The other thing that has emerged, I think, at least to my mind, is this: it is much clearer that when one has translated the model from one situation to another and has allowed for the reciprocity, one sees that there is in fact much more reciprocity in the original situation of counsellor and client than I at least had thought. You see what I mean, Martin?'

'I know exactly what you mean.'

'Which is interesting, it seems to me, because I think that one's general image of the relationship of counsellor and client *is* one of dependency and so on, whereas what our conclusion makes clearer is that the process between counsellor and client is fundamentally at the level of two human beings struggling with each other at a task in which *both* have to learn — which, I think, you indicated at one point, and that's partly why you rejected my terms "inferior" and "superior". In other words, there's feedback.'

'Yes', Dr. Gregory replied. 'I must say — and I'm not saying this to exonerate myself — that I never had the feeling, consciously (perhaps I had it unconsciously to some extent), of some superiority. The expression I always use with my clients is: "We have to work together." It's a question of a *common* working through of problems, of questions, and I'm very much aware of the enormous enrichment of my life that comes from my being permitted to do this. So although I was not conscious that the process was reciprocal in the sense which you have now made explicit, and which is probably more so in the case of a consciously conducted *Gespräch* between friends, I always felt that the inflow of experience, the encounter with destiny, the entry into a wider life which came to me from my clients as well as from my friends was something that enriches and sustains me. I feel particularly privileged to be able to enter into the thinking of young people because they bring ideas, impulses and inclinations which are quite different from anything I've experienced before. For example, their concern with events in Africa, Asia, India was totally unknown to us when we were young.'

'I quite agree.'

'The impulses of helpfulness, compassion, participation were unknown to us, not because we were bad or stupid people but because our life and our world were very narrow, very restricted. You see, the twentieth century which broke everything up had not, so to speak, fully started to do that. And if you read a book like Stefan Zweig's *The World of Yesterday,* the first few chapters, then you will get an admirable description of this restricted, dusty, twilight atmosphere, of really being cut off from the totality of life. And in this sense, you see, I experience a tremendous inflow.'

'Yes, I completely agree with you, Martin. And to be more conscious of this is important in at least two respects. First of all, in regard to one's own attitude, which is therefore much more one of humility. But even more importantly, one is perhaps more conscious of trying to communicate this sense to the other person in a counselling situation. For I have certainly found that so often people put me on a pedestal and say, at least in extreme cases, "But I'm giving you nothing". This is very bad for their self-esteem, and, you know — I think of one person in particular — to the extent that I'm aware that she's giving me something, I can in principle help her self-esteem. But it's the last thing they think when they feel bad or rejected, and capable of giving nothing. I think that it could be important to try to communicate this sense that, as you say, we're trying to work through something together, that we counsellors are receiving something, that we're privileged.'

'It's absolutely true. You see, as you're talking, I become conscious of the fact that in former years, as distinct from the present, people often said this to me. And I can't tell you, nor do I know, why it has changed — probably because my basic feelings have changed, probably also because the difference between a priest and a doctor is very great: a priest is very much more an object and a person to be revered. A doctor, you see, or a therapist, if he tunes in in the right way, will, I think, be able to — "project" is again a bad word, but you know what I mean — will come across to the other person as a fellow human being, and he can then indicate, primarily, of course, in his silent inner attitude of listening and receiving, but also, occasionally, in a more explicit way, his appreciation of what he's allowed to listen to. This reciprocal relationship can be established and gently emphasised. But that is in contrast to what some therapists think, in terms of life as well as in terms of a *Gespräch*. Reciprocity, that is a fundamental thing. And the more the client becomes aware of it, and the more he feels deep down that the counsellor is just someone who shares things with him as a person who has experienced his own difficulties, his own troubles, which he has tried to solve, and that by speaking to him the client gives him something which the counsellor receives as a gift, the more the therapeutic encounter will gain, and the results will, of course, improve. So shall we leave it there?'

'I think you've made your case, Martin!'

'Well, you put me on my mettle.'

notes

1. David Stafford-Clark *Psychiatry for Students* 5th edn. (London, 1979).

dialogue 3: relationship and solitude

'I've been thinking a great deal about what you said in our two previous discussions, Martin, and allowing it to turn my experiences and thoughts over and over, like a plough with the earth in the autumn. I don't know whether I've been more fascinated by your analysis of the process of counselling into seven stages or by your subsequent deepening of the significance of this process so as to see it as one, but privileged, example of the human dialogue as such. As a result of this pondering, however, I've come up with a problem which, from one point of view represents a stop, but which, from another point of view, can be the starting-point of yet further insight, and which I should therefore very much like to discuss with you. I can broach the problem I have in mind like this. You have, if I remember rightly, at least once quoted one of Rilke's lovely sayings to the effect that relationship is a matter of two solitudes greeting, touching and protecting each other, haven't you? '

'Yes', replied Dr. Gregory, 'it is another of my favourite sayings, I quote it quite often.'

'Well now, Martin', I continued, 'I first came across this particular saying myself indirectly, via a beautiful book of memoirs written by Lawrence Whistler, entitled *The Initials in the Heart*. He, you may know, was the glass engraver, married to a promising young actress who died in giving birth to their second child, and he wrote this book some years later in order to achieve some tranquility by celebrating what was obviously a rare and quite special relationship. And towards the end of the book he quotes this saying of Rilke, but added something critical: "This appealed to our romantic side, and she quoted it, sensing and believing also that love can go further than that. The solitude is not sealed, somehow it is penetrable." Now what was important to his wife and to himself in recalling this comment on Rilke's saying was what he called the "penetrability" of people to each other, and this is also the way in which this saying of Rilke is immediately relevant to our discussion to date, in so far as all these reflections deal with the relational side of our lives. My problem, however, is that there is also this other side to our lives, the fact that Rilke referred to when he said that what greeted, touched and protected each other, the subjects of the relationship, were two *solitudes*. Isn't there ultimately within us what you yourself have well termed an island where we are alone with ourselves? Isn't there, therefore, an ineluctable solitude, that solitude from and within which we face death, so that we can even, as the earlier Heidegger said, be described as beings *zum Tode*, beings for death? But, if this is the case, then, so my thoughts have gone so far, another way of describing what life is about is that it consists in a polarity between, on the one hand, the real need for other people, the need to reach out to them, to become as "penetrable" as possible to them, in ways that may be infinitely variable, such as we have been discussing so far, and, on the other hand, this inevitable and final solitude. Thus even in a life-long relationship life, there is a continuous inter-play between these poles of relationship and solitude. Now that's as far as my own thinking has gone so far, but in so far it's valid, it's the element of solitude that sets up the polarity which I should like to go on to grapple with. Do you see?'

'Yes, indeed, Marcus, and I think that you've already gone very far. May I remind you of one of the first things you said when we met, and this is that what attracted you to enter the Order was this basic movement between activity and withdrawing into contemplation. And I think it is probably one of the basic laws of living altogether, even one of the basic laws of life in the biological and physiological sense, that we need to return to our own centre. It is like sleeping in regard to wakefulness, so that in the end we desire sleep in order to be awake again. Similarly you have the same kind of basic law of going inward, taking in and then pouring out operative in breathing.'

'In the heart?', I asked.

'Yes, in the breathing itself, systole and diastole. So there is no question of this not being true. Loneliness can never by anything one-sided, in one direction, such that you return to yourself so to speak once and for all.'

'I'm glad that you corroborate my view, Martin, but your use of the word "loneliness" introduces another note, and brings me back to my problem, especially as loneliness is where the problem of solitude becomes more practical, more applied and more concerned with therapy. Even I have found that quite a lot of my work is concerned with trying to reconcile people to their loneliness. However, one way in which I have tried to come to terms with this myself — for myself and for other people — is to see loneliness as being something very distinct from solitude. On such a view, loneliness is an unhappy state, but probably a transitional state, almost an ordeal you have to go through, as part of your grappling with solitude, as a way through to solitude. I should, therefore, distinguish very sharply between loneliness and solitude, and I think that I remember your saying that the Austrian philosopher and theologian Lotz has written a book to this effect, hasn't he? That loneliness is the ordeal, the purgation for, almost the initiation into solitude?'.

'Yes, he has', replied Dr. Gregory. 'He has written a wonderful book about solitude, and he does indeed distinguish between loneliness and solitude. I believe the terms he uses in German are *Vereinsamung,* which is the equivalent of loneliness, and *Einsamkeit.'*

'That's an ordinary German word, isn't it?' I asked.

'Oh yes. And this *Einsamkeit* is creative solitude.'

'It is. In this solitude you're very much in touch, you're in touch with all manner of things, therefore implicitly with everything else.'

'Exactly', continued Dr. Gregory. 'It's the artist's, the mystic's solitude. Because once you have got through to this solitude, broken through to your true centre, which is the essential implication of the word, you are no longer alone, because in some mysterious way your whole being widens and begins to make contact with, begins to flow into, begins to identify not only with creatures but with creation, with the creative world altogether. In something I've read, I no longer know where, this state is described as consisting in an identification with the trees, with the souls of trees, with the storms, with the grass, and of course with all living things. It depends, of course, on the intensity of this stage, it can be comparatively narrow, and it can be extremely wide and expansive. But here again you have the same basic law, the basic rhythm. Once you have achieved this journey inwards to the very end, you are already on the way up, on the journey outward, and a greater journey outward than you have every undertaken before, than you can ever undertake in ordinary life — I mean in the life of a purely physical condition, where you are confined.'

'I quite agree, and I'm sure that is so', I said, 'because I think I've glimpsed it. It's only a glimpse, if only because it's also a progressive thing, it's a rhythm, it's part of the rhythm of life and of the individual, and it's a rhythm which deepens, doesn't it, and which extends throughout the system and personality as one grows older.'

'Yes, exactly, Marcus. You see, as you grow older, quite naturally even your physical possibilities of expanding outwards become much more limited. For example, you cannot walk so far or so fast, you cannot exert your body so much, and more and more the people who surrounded you, your friends, either are somewhere else or are dead, or some such. But the more the outer world contracts, the more — ideally, at least — the more your inner world can and should expand, provided, of course, you have not developed a habit of clinging to the outer structure of life. You must be prepared for the move, and you must be on the way as far as this journey inwards is concerned. And then there are simply no limits to the scope and to the newness of your experience.'

'I can see that, Martin, though I'm obviously not at that stage myself. It seems to me that at an earlier phase of life, say middle age, I think that there is a possibility of a slightly different emphasis, and this is that to the extent that you can get in touch with your inner centre, your contemplative withdrawal is — again ideally, and for some — not only very compatible with an increased activity but at a certain point occurs in the very midst of activity, so that the rhythm becomes much more subtle, it is interiorised. You talked about this communion with the trees, and so on, and about the experience of going into the country for relaxation, of getting away from it all, as we say. This is an everyday version of the pantheistic, Wordsworthian sort of experience, but it seems to me that this is in itself only symbolic, that the natural, stable, continuing and self-renewing world of nature is in itself a symbol of the creative principle. And I think that ideally one could be in touch with that creative principle of the universe, something vaster than oneself, the origin of one's own and every other person's origins, in the midst of bustle and the city. I think that this contact is extremely difficult to sustain, and that, practically speaking, one may need these periods of physical withdrawal. But I also think that there comes a point where activity and contemplation are almost fused, because one has broken through. One needs to sleep, one needs to withdraw, the rhythm of life is the same and yet it expresses itself differently. To the outsider this person is almost ceaselessly active and energetic, and yet at the same time he is deeply contemplative and is only active because he is contemplative.'

'Yes, I think that is profoundly true, Marcus, and I think it has a very important bearing on the work which we try to do. As you say, you can remain in touch with the centre, at least once you have reached it; this is a pre-condition in bustle and activity. But I think it is absolutely essential that once you have touched that, you consciously re-establish the centre in any human encounter, whatever your previous activities were. So you have these two dimensions when you are opposite another person who presents you with a problem: on the one hand, you withdraw into the centre of silent openness, silent listening, you are in a way entirely contemplative, on the other hand, you are entirely turned outwards, to receive the other.'

'This is that dynamic relaxation to which you referred before?,' I asked.

'This is dynamic relaxation. And I think that in ordinary life, you also ideally need this balance, or fusion of these two elements, in order to cope with life. And in actual fact, the more you have established a centre, free of memories, concepts, and the like, in an impersonal way...'

'A very dispossessed, unpossessive way?', I interjected.

'Yes, in a dispossessed, an unpossessive way; and the more you have established this, this kind of room, like a holy of holies...'

'Like Rilke's *Weltinnenraum*, the world's inner space?', I again ventured to interpose;

'Yes, indeed, then the more the other person or experience can enter.'

'I must say I absolutely agree with all that, Martin. You're describing, in your own idiom, the inwardness of the schema, the abstract schema of what John Macmurray in his idiom referred to as the rhythm of withdrawal and return. And I think it is also what the Hebrew psalmist meant when he referred to the man who goes out and comes in. It's a very frequent description of the human predicament and condition so that the classical Hebrew often refers to men who come in and who go out. It represents a very simple and particular way of hitting off the same rhythm, which through this very particularity is in the end nothing less than the rhythm of the universe itself. At the same time, all that we've said, with the various qualifications we've put in, means to say that this abstract schema of withdrawal and return can in fact take very many different concrete forms. It no doubt needs to be sustained by physical withdrawal, at least in the period of training, of initiation, and perhaps always to some extent, since as physical, mortal creatures we need these periods of acted-out withdrawal and return. But, granted that, the abstract schema seems to be able to take very many different forms, according to one's temperament and one's age and phase of life.'

'Absolutely, yes. And although, as you say, it can take ever so many individual forms according to age, disposition, temperament, circumstances, conditions of life, it must first of all be *established*. It must also be *maintained*, and in my experience it requires an enormous amount of perseverance, patience and tenacity. For this reason, therefore, it has someting of the character of a discipline.'

'It has a spiritual reference, you mean, Martin, it is a spiritual discipline?'

'Yes', Dr. Gregory went on. 'But it is a discipline of great practical and therapeutic importance. Most, if not all the people I meet get into a state of crisis or distress because they have not learned to fight their way back into, not loneliness, but what we have now referred to as creative solitude.'

'That's exactly one of my practical difficulties in therapeutic counselling work. I'm thinking of two or three people I'm dealing with at the moment, and if I reflect on it, I now realise that what I'm trying to do is to enable them to enter into their own solitude. Yet the drag of dependence and of activism and of compulsion to be connected with other people in different ways is so strong in such cases that you have to be very patient, and very, very gentle. And it may be very difficult in regard to such people to indicate the possibility that they have to find a systematic way of continuing to find their solitude. The most I have been able to do with two of the people I have in mind is to indicate to them that the answer is within. The next step would then be for them gradually to realise that there is some form of life particularly appropriate to them in which they can express and consolidate this. Very few people, as you say, I think, can do this, because once they are over the crisis they almost inevitably relapse.'

'Yes, that is absolutely true, Marcus. I've recently had the case of a very fine woman who is completely identified with and absorbed and overwhelmed by an environment which is not a very genuine environment for her, and as a result she is constantly being pulled away from her own centre. I've tried various things, but she is almost always pulled away again. And I feel now with her and with very many people, which I've felt only recently, that what we have to do with such people is not simply to try to help them with ways to solve their problems but to teach them an inner discipline, which is again a spiritual thing. For example, we have to show them how to achieve a certain measure of detachment. When you mention the word detachment to a person it sounds quite wonderful but it also sounds very strange. They wonder what it's about, and even if they understand what it is, they do not know how to achieve it. This is why my own thinking has rather gone beyond counselling as a form of helping people to deal with personal problems to counselling as a form of helping people establish a disciplined inner way of life, where they can achieve detachment, where they can achieve creative solitude. And that's a different matter altogether.'

'Yes, that again echoes my own experience very exactly, and in a quite particular sort of way in connection with the two people I'm thinking about in so far as they are both women. They've made great progress, they're much more self-possessed, they're much more able to live with themselves, much more free of infantile fantasies and dependencies. Nevertheless they've both got an almost *idée fixe* about having a man. Now I feel that what is fundamentally in question here is some extremely important need to relate, but also that in so far as this is expressed in terms of *having* to have a man in their lives this very need constitutes a block.'

'Yes, I follow you, Marcus, and can I say something to that very briefly? Generally speaking, then, I have yet to see a woman who does not need to have a man in her life, but the essential thing in my opinion is that for many women it is not absolutely necessary and sometimes not even desirable to have a man in terms of a lover or a husband, but to have a man who represents the guiding, manly, spiritual element. It may be a priest, it may be a doctor, and you must know from your experience how women can come and fasten on to the therapist or the priest because he is a man. Now there are two aspects in such a case. On the one hand, her emotions, her erotic, her sexual feelings will tend to flow towards him, but woe to him if he confuses matters, then he is a fallen idol. On the other hand, it is a fact that the life of a woman can — to a very great extent, not fully, of course — be fulfilled by a kind of relationship to a spiritual guide, a man to whom she looks up. It must be a man, because if there is no man she will again become mannish, and that's a very bad thing.'

'She becomes what Jung would call the animus-ridden woman?', I asked.

'Yes, she becomes absolutely indigestible, aggressive, self-dependent, self-righteous, or whatever.''

'So, Martin, the important thing for a therapist in such a situation is first of all to be quite clear himself so that he can as far as possible gradually communicate the distinction between himself as a man and as an archetypal figure. And, of course, this very way of formulating the question is very androcentric and so immediately raises the further, correlative question as to what a man needs in regard to a woman. But that's another subject in itself and we haven't time to go into that today.'

'No, Marcus, indeed not. But may I just dot an "i" in regard to that first question? A man who deals with a woman should not, in my experience and thinking, deny that he is a man.'

'No, he can't become disincarnate, he is a person, a real human being, and therefore a sexed being.'

'Yes, and I make a point of telling women — and, for that matter, telling men something different — that they are very nice, or attractive or beautiful women, or whatever it is. But the fact that the therapist is able to control inappropriate immediate responses and, moreover, to indicate a different and even a higher level is something that people are really waiting for, they are still waiting for it.'

'I have to go now, Martin, but may I just say before I do that to me the upshot of our discussion this morning is that true dialogue presupposes solitude, which turns out to be a spiritual matter, that reflection on the nature of dialogue leads on to the need to consider as it were the spirituality of counselling, and that we really need at some stage to undertake such a discussion together.'

'I should indeed very much like to do that at some time, Marcus, I'll gather my thoughts around this topic and look forward to that.'

dialogue 4: woman and man

'Martin, I said last time that the dynamic of our conversations so far seems to have been in the direction of going on to discuss the spiritual dimension of counselling. Just before the end of our last dialogue, however, we found ourselves by the inner development of that exploration together raising the question of what a woman means for a man, by way of correlative to the question of what a man means to a woman. Now I think that this is so important a topic, especially at the level on which you were beginning to talk, that I should like to discuss that this evening. For I think that very few of us get tired of discussing the relationship of man and woman in their mutual counter-sexuality, and yet there is a perhaps even greater fascination in that aspect of the subject on which you began to lift a veil last time, namely, the way in which man and woman have a spiritual significance for each other. I wonder whether you could develop that a little, and, in particular, tell me what you think about the spiritual significance of a woman for a man.'

'Yes', replied Dr. Gregory, 'I should indeed like to discuss this with you, but it is rather unexplored territory for me, you know, and so I should prefer to start with some sort of framework. And although, as you know by now, my whole temperament makes me reluctant to begin with a merely bare and abstract structure, nothing else is available at the moment, and so I'll tell you the way I've tried to organise my thinking on what is an enormously complex subject. Now, I think that when a man meets a woman, he meets her on four levels. These four levels are simply, (a) the purely physical level, (b) the biological, (c) the emotional, psychological, and (d) the ego level, in a relationship with another leading into the realm of the purely spiritual. You see, I think that we men need women at all these levels. At the same time, on all these levels we can, I believe, encounter, on the one hand, a very negative image, a destructive, dark image, and, on the other, a radiant, life-giving, perhaps even a sublime image. I am not very conversant with Jungian psychology but I have recently read that Jung also distinguished these two basic responses, or two basic qualities of encounter between men and women, namely, on the one hand, one which is positive and, on the other hand, one which is negative. Hence while the one is life-giving, the other is destructive, in certain cases almost death-giving. Now that's as far as I've got in my very abstract structuring of the subject, these four levels and these two basic polar opposites. Can you take anything out of this?'

'Well, Martin, what you have done so far is to distinguish between the physical, the biological, the emotional and the spiritual levels, haven't you?'

'Yes.'

'Do you, however, remember how in a previous *Gespräch*, which we did not record, we were talking about what we paradoxically called sexuality without sex and on that occasion you distinguished three levels, the physical, the emotional and the spiritual. Then you 'phoned me up, I think it was the next day, and you said that you would like to introduce a fourth term, not only what you then called *sexus, eros* and *agapé* but *philia;* and you also added that this seemed to correspond very closely to the fourfold distinction made by C.S. Lewis in his *Four Loves,* in terms of affection, friendship, eros and charity. Do you remember that?'

'Yes, Marcus.'

'Now the first question that comes to my mind is to what extent these four sorts of love which you distinguished previously correspond to the four levels you have just distinguished, namely, the physical, the biological, the emotional and the spiritual?'

'Yes, it's a little difficult to put these things into exact correspondence. On the other hand, I don't think it's too difficult. The purely physical relationship is, of course, what corresponds to *sexus.* The biological relationship corresponds to *eros,* but in my opinion it also includes maternal feelings, protective feelings, supportive feelings. *Eros* is not necessarily suffused with *sexus,* though we have to bear in mind that these things completely interpenetrate. Therefore when we come to the ego level, the level of the self, the woman appears to a man as a companion, and a friend, in a relationship which may be desexualised and de-eroticised. And it is into this relationship, of course, that *agapé* can enter, although *agapé* is quite obviously a much higher form of loving again than *philia*. All these things interpenetrate, and can move from one level to another. There is no doubt that a total relationship between a man and a woman should, if at all possible, encompass all these levels.'

'All that is very interesting and useful, Martin, but surely you have now introduced three classifications and not merely two: firstly, the classification with which you began this morning, in terms of the physical, the biological, the emotional and the spiritual; secondly, your previous one in terms of the sexual, the erotic, the friendly, and the spiritual; and then, thirdly, C.S. Lewis' fourfold distinction in terms of affection, friendship, eros and charity. To my mind, however, these four classifications don't all coincide, they're not completely correlated: if you drew up a parallel list you would find that they didn't correspond. But in one sense any such discrepancy doesn't matter since the different classifications represent different attempts to find an adequate, shall we call it typology of love. And what is important is the attempt to understand the subject represented by any such typology. Besides, even the most adequate typology would still leave us in rather an abstract realm and what I'm really interested in is something more on the lines of what you had said about the relationship between man and woman the other way round. You know, just as a woman in some sense needs to have a man in his archetypal aspect as a guide, such as we began to discuss last time, what is it that a man needs in a woman in that sort of perspective? This is a different framework of reference, I suppose it's a more Jungian way of looking at it. It's really a question of the symbolism of the mutual relationship. So the question is whether there is any equivalent to the man being a guide to the woman the other way round?'

'Yes, absolutely equivalent', responded Dr. Gregory. 'You see, in terms of practical life and of a successful marriage in which people grow old, it's almost inevitable that the sexual attraction diminishes, often vanishes altogether, and that equally the erotic feelings vanish or at least recede. Not, in my opinion, that this is a particularly desirable "victory", and I often say to my clients that it's by no means a good thing that a sexual and an erotic relationship in a marriage should be discarded. It is, however, natural that in the course of time and the course of development *philia,* the aspect of friendship, should come to preponderate more and more.'

'The proportion changes, Martin?'

'The proportion completely changes. I think that a man who has lived a happy marriage with a woman finds that she has become predominantly a friend, that is to say a person to whom he turns in need and to share with. It can also happen that there is a relationship with another woman. Men have told me about it, and in such a case there are not sexually erotic feelings at all. There may have been such sexual feelings at some time, of a more or less episodic character, which then by an organic process, so to speak, have been worked through and left behind so that the woman becomes a trusted friend and counsellor to the man. In such a case you have *philia* too. Then the other way in which the relationship between a man and woman grows beyond the earlier stages, and this is the really important thing for our present purpose, is in terms of the feeling a woman has in regard to religion, and you are probably more aware of this than I am. Instinctively, psychologically, almost biologically this is different from the corresponding attitude to religion which a man has. A man is much more burdened with his physical body, is much more burdened with his intellect, is perhaps much more burdened with his passions and other preoccupations. A woman often has a kind of inborn religious genius, and this is why you see many more women in churches. I can certainly say in my own case that my wife Emma was always a person who was religiously, intuitively much more open than I was and has given me great help in these matters. Now when we begin to enter this sphere of religion and true openness to the spiritual world, then we come into the realm of *agapé.* It is in this way that, if you have a woman who represents *philia* to you and if she is also spiritually open and developed, then she will also be a bearer of *agapé* for you. Here we are talking about the almost ideal woman, and as I talk I think particularly of Goethe since he has portrayed women in his works who were ideal representatives of womanhood in the sense in which I am talking at the moment.'

'The eternal feminine?'

'Yes, the eternal feminine in its redeemed completeness where sexuality has been transformed and become sublime, virginal. Here the maternal element has remained, and love as *philia* is also present, but a sublime inspirational quality which relates this person to the divine world has supervened. In Goethe's work Iphigenia was such a character, and in *Wilhelm Meister* there was likewise the sublime Makarie, typically so-called *makarie*, from the Greek *makarios, makaria...*'

'meaning blessed, happy', I supplied,

'yes, blessed, a person who is sublime: maternal, loving and at the same time endowed with a spirituality which, as Goethe describes it, makes her a being who lives with the cosmos. He describes in detail the way she remains an incarnate being and yet moves in the realm of the stars. All this is wonderfully summed up at the end of Faust, the second Faust. Here it is one of the *patres* who looks up at the heavens towards the *Mater gloriosa*, Maria, (Mary, of course) and he addresses her with these four words: *"Jungfrau, Mutter, Königin, Göttin"*, "Virgin, Mother, Queen, Goddess". That is the ultimate image, the total image of redeemed womanhood, which of course in the most idealised form would then represent a spiritual guidance.'

'That is much more the sort of thing I wanted to hear your views about, Martin, because you are now saying that a woman can become a guide to a man where you had formerly said that a man can be a guide to a woman. This is so deep and subtle that I should like to put the question in another form. Even granted that this sort of friendship between the man and woman can gradually gain a predominance over the other levels, the physical and sexual, even the erotic and emotional, is there something specific about the mutual contributions a man and a woman can make to each other? I think that you have already suggested that there is. Only it is no longer so much a matter of a sexual difference but rather of what we should have to call a *gender* difference. This is what I am feeling for, do you see? And you have already suggested that in the give and take between a man and a woman in their very friendship, even in their spiritual communion, there remains something which is not undifferentiated and neutral and transcendent, since they remain profoundly sexed — or gendered, that would perhaps be the better word.'

'Yes, gendered', agreed Dr. Gregory.

'There therefore seems to be a specific difference even at the spiritual level, let alone at that of friendship. So is there a contradiction or a confusion, or a very interesting paradox, in saying that in their very specificity as man and woman they can be, in different ways perhaps, guides to each other? And another classical example of this would, of course, be Dante's *Divina Comedia* where it is first of all a man, Virgil, who is the guide, but in the final stages, the woman Beatrice.'

'Very true', agreed Dr. Gregory.

'So I suppose that would be the Italian, Romance equivalent of the Germanic legend, myth, wouldn't it?'

'Yes, indeed.'

'So', I continued, 'there is what in one sense is an abstract problem but what in another sense is, I think, a very concrete problem about relating these two sorts of ways of being a guide: the way a man is a guide to a woman, which you began to explore the last time, and the way a woman is a guide to a man, which we are exploring now. Do you see?'

'I do see exactly what you mean, Marcus. I think that the difference is fundamentally in the quality of guidance and spiritual substance that is transmitted. I think that it is very characteristic that in the example you gave yourself it is Beatrice who is the guide at the end. Similarly in *Faust* Gretchen and the *mater gloriosa* are guides at the end. The reason, I believe, is that the whole constitution of a woman is much less earth-bound than that of a man. You know, her, if I may so call it, incarnation is less dense and less intense, is much more *spiritually open*. She has something which a man rarely has in ordinary life, unless he is an exceptional person, and this is an intuitive, an almost *prophetic ability*, the quality of being a sybil. I can give you a very simple example from my own life. I easily get worried about things, as I have told you, about certain family situations, and then I look at my wife, Emma, and when I see that she is calm, I take my cue from her, you see, because long experience has convinced me, as it has also convinced our youngest daughter who is still at home, that by virtue of being so youthful, light and feminine and spiritually open she has some intuitive faculties of knowing what is going on, which we haven't got. A man in his thinking, in his type of awareness, is much more centred, much more practical, more focussed, more committed to making exact and truthful and precise statements, much more committed to organised work, to intellectual work than a woman as such is. A woman often appears to be connected in a mysterious way with life and the life-forces in their lower as well as in their higher forms. You see, in the sense in which I'm talking about men and women at the moment, what is characteristic of each is expressed in their very bodily shape and structure. The physique of a man has a harder structure corresponding to his more focussed personality, whereas a woman's very shape has something of a rounded fulness about it that suggests a circuit of vital feelings. As a result the man's vitality, life-force is at a much lower level than that of the woman who feels and knows deep within her that she will generally survive her husband. Therefore also when it comes to crisis, and particularly the last crisis of dying and death, the natural gift of woman, her natural relatedness to life as a whole, and especially to the spiritual dimension of life, comes into its own, provided she has allowed this development to take place within her. This can be an enormous comfort and help to a man. She will tend to approach crisis situations much more calmly than he, she will often show a tremendous endurance far beyond *his* possibilities. And so far as dying is concerned, she may be able to face the death of her companion with an equanimity a man cannot produce in the reverse situation. One of the most wonderful examples I know of is provided by the case of the German poet Christian Morgenstern. I wonder whether you've heard of him? He is often compared with Edward Lear on account of his own nonsense verses, but he was a deeper person. He was a disciple of Rudolf Steiner, in all liberty, and died of tuburculosis at the early age of 42. His wife Margareta was sitting with him at his bedside when he came to die, which he did in the end very quickly. Looking at him, she saw him going, and said *"Kein Schmerz, nur Freude"*, "No pain, only joy". With these words sounding in his ears, he passed over. I think that's fantastic. I think that only a woman could do that. Here you have, I believe, a sublime example of a spiritual guide — of a woman of this earth who will help a man to pass over the threshold into the next life in this way.'

'So, you are saying, Martin, that what a woman means for a man, what attracts a man towards a woman as a guide, is her ability to guide him through the latter part of life and particularly through death? And, further, that this quality, is however, only the explicit form of what he has somehow always seen to be implicit even in the earlier part of life in so far as she is more in touch with what you call the life-forces?'

'Exactly.'

'So that a woman is indeed a guide to a man, just as a man is a guide to a woman, though presumably in different and complementary ways?'

'Absolutely complementary, Marcus. She will not intensify his consciousness, in the way that a man can activate and intensify a woman's consciousness of herself and her awareness of the world. But he will turn to her for his liberation — and there's always this quality of liberation, because when he meets her he will be liberated, in many ways, as in the act of love, freèd from being so strongly imprisoned in his body, being so strongly centred in his emotions and his intellect. He will be lifted up, led onto a higher, less conscious, more spiritual level of awareness.'

'And he will not do that for her, Martin?', I puzzled.

'He will do it, but in a different way. He will do it for her by communicating to her something of his consciousness, of his earthly awareness in so far as she lacks this. Do you see what I'm trying to say? It's very difficult to express.'

'It is, and I'm trying to understand; yet I also feel that you're onto something as vital as it's subtle — the question of the specific contribution and complement each has to give the other. Because I don't think that you're saying, are you, Martin, that it's the function of the woman as it were to lift up the man but not the function of the man to life up the woman? You're also maintaining that the man has to "lift up" the woman too, even, as you say, in the act of love, but in a different kind of way.'

'In a different kind of way, yes. The whole constitution of a woman is less earth-bound, less bound to everyday consciousness, so that when she meets a man she wakens into his sort of consciousness; she will become much more aware of herself. I'll give you an example: a woman is according to her psychic being given to confabulation, she can invent her own truth. Now many women want to overcome this, and they do overcome it, in confrontation with a man whose consciousness is focussed in quite a different sort of way. Whatever he is, a man is not a liar. The most truthful people I've ever met were in prison, when I used to work with prisoners. So there is an awakening, but into a different sphere of awareness and truth.'

'Is it an awakening into a greater concreteness, application, Martin?'

'Yes, exactly.'

'So the difference is between — I'm groping for adequate words — between something like diffusion and concentration, to put it abstractly?'

'Yes, indeed. You see, a woman tends to lack this power to focus her whole being into clarity, purposefulness, and so on, out of a state of comparative diffusion. A man's problem, on the other hand, is to overcome his burdened, concentrated being, to be liberated into a level of comparative diffusion, which should not, however, remain diffusion but should become an awareness beyond his ordinary one.'

'I've been captivated by what you've been saying, Martin, but I've also been struggling to understand the finesse of your thinking. So I wonder whether I might try to attempt a crass summary in my own terms. It so happens that I was again reading the *Summa Theologica* of St Thomas Aquinas recently. In the passage I was perusing he's talking about the distinction between what he calls *intellectus* and *ratio,* roughly intuitive understanding and discursive reasoning in the sense of ratiocination, working out. What he says is that the human being, precisely as human being, as distinct from the angel, does not have an immediate and simple perception of the truth, he has to work towards it, work it out, and that is what reasoning, ratiocination, is about. Then, in one of his beautiful *obiter dicta,* he goes on to say that we ratiocinate in order to *eke out the defects of our intuition.* Now the point of bringing in St Thomas Aquinas here is that if we equate the intuitive with the feminine quality and the ratiocinative with the masculine quality then what the woman has to give the man is this more spiritual, synchronic, intuition, whereas what a man has to give a woman is the working out, the diachronic, the application of the intuition.'

'That's exactly it, Marcus.'

'So that they each bring the other complementary aspects of the one human capacity of feeling-borne understanding. This would tie up everything you've said, I think; it would do justice to the specific, gender-differentiated contribution of each, whilst also to some extent explaining the paradox that each can be a guide to the other, in their different way.'

'Yes, that's an excellent summary.'

'But, just one more thing — which may then lead us on to yet another chapter! If this is in any way an adequate way of summarising your thinking, then how are we to relate all this to the wonderfully suggestive thesis of Esther Harding, a very considerable early disciple of Jung? You know how in her marvellous book, *The Way of All Women,* she maintains that the specifically feminine thing is *eros,* which is her Jungian way of rendering the feeling, relational element in human beings, whereas the specifically masculine thing is what she correspondingly calls *logos.* What the woman has specifically to give is *eros,* whilst what the man specifically has to give is *logos,* and these are on this view their complementary functions. Now that is a different way again of articulating, conceptualising the difference, isn't it, Martin?'

'We haven't time to discuss this fully now, but I tend to think it's simply a difference of terminology. If we were able to discuss it more thoroughly, I think that we should conclude that this represents a different way of saying the same thing.'

'That intuition, in your enlarged and subtle way of talking about it, is the same thing as Esther Harding's *eros,* and that man's reason as I have defined it, that power of focussed, applied thinking is the sense of Esther Harding's *logos?*'

'I should perhaps myself add that this intuition is transfigured, metamorphosed. It's a soul-quality, in so far as the woman's capacity for feeling is rooted in her soul-being, which is much more deeply related to life and its mysteries. In this sense, it's much more than an intellectual thing, it's soaked in feeling. There the whole thing becomes one.'

'Well, I think that we've meandered more than I had envisaged, and perhaps we should now go back and straighten out some of the loops and turns. But then we might lose a great deal of the vitality and interest of the joint search.'

'Yes, you confronted me with an extremely subtle question, namely, the difference in quality of guidance as between a man and a woman and, quite frankly, I was (a) rather tired tonight, and (b) not prepared for this precise problem. But I think that we have in the end come up with something valuable, and I particularly appreciate your summary.'

'Well, I find what you said quite fascinating, Martin, because you've made me revise, if not reverse, many of my previous ways of thinking about what a man and a woman stand for. For I had taken women to be earth-bound, and you've shown me that this quality is much more subtle than I had conceived. She *is* in an important sense earth-bound, but she is also in an even more important sense liberated from the earth, almost transcendent in her vitality.'

'Absolutely, and I think one can experience this in a very simple way. To speak personally, you know that I often feel tired and then I leave my study in order to go down into the living-room and sit down with my wife and daughter. Then there's something that as it were radiates from these women, which is a positive balm for me, the very thing I've been missing and of which I feel I've been depleted.'

'And let's hope that you have a corresponding and complementary effect on them, Martin!'.

'Well, I hope so!'

'Well, Martin, that's really come down to the particular and the concrete. We started rather aloft, abstractly, but now we've come down to earth, back to the living-room!'

'Yes, indeed. I'm very happy that is should be so...'

dialogue 5: the stages of
the spiritual path

'Well, Martin', I said this particular morning, 'we must have been discussing matters that are very close to our hearts on and off over some five years, and in that time you have explained to me your ideas, your evolving ideas, on the stages of counselling. A little bit further in our acquaintance you developed your ideas about the counselling session as a privileged example of the archetype of the human *Gespräch*. We've also discussed the subject of relationship and solitude, and that of woman and man, and in both discussions we've found ourselves uncovering a spiritual dimension. But what we have not done is to record together a dialogue on the spiritual path, on the stages of spiritual growth, and I know that this is an extremely important thing for you, in its own right but also in its relationship to counselling. So I should be very grateful if today you could recapitulate your ideas on the spiritual path as such, independently of the counselling, as it were. You understand? Then if I may, I shall just come in with questions or requests for clarification, as may be, alright?'

'Yes, as you say, quite some time has passed since we began discussing all these things,' Dr. Gregory replied, 'and I'm inclined to forget what I've said before. So you may find that what I try to say today will be different in many ways, but not in any fundamental way.

Now, I think I'd better start with a statement about what we might call the essential structure of what I feel is the spiritual path. And I believe that nobody has stated it more clearly than the great teacher, a great yogi, who was, so many believe, the greatest teacher of the spiritual path, namely, the Buddha. And I encountered this particular formula about the spiritual path and its structure in the so-called, in English you would say, the "death-gospel" of the

Buddha, that is to say, the narrative of the events of the Buddha's life as he in his wandering with his monks approaches death. Now at this time, by way of a supreme testament and message to his monks, it seems to me, he repeated over and over again one formula, the formula about the being and structure of the spiritual path. Naturally, apart from the formula, many other details are added, for it is of course enveloped in the events of his life during the last few months. But I should like to read you this because I have never found anything else quite as revealing as this. He says — I'll read it in the German version in which I myself came across it, and then you can translate it':

> *"Und so redete der Heilige....den Jüngern in reicher Ausführlichkeit über das Wesen der heiligen Wahrheit, immer wieder ihnen zeigend: So ist sittliche Selbsterziehung, so meditative Versenkung, so wahre höhere Erkenntnis. Nur von sittlicher Selbsterziehung getragen und geläutert ist Meditation ertragreich und segensvoll, nur von Meditation getragen und geläutert ist Erkenntnis ertragreich und segensvoll, und von solcher Erkenntnis durchdrungen und geläutert wird der Geist frei."*

'May I just check with you that I understand this, for it's extraordinarily dense, and I want to make sure that I've got it right. It means:

> "And so the holy one spoke to his disciples in rich detail about the essence of holy truth, indicating to them over and over again: This is ethical discipline, this is meditative recollection, this is true higher knowledge. It is only if it is supported and refined by ethical discipline that meditation is fruitful and blessed, it is only if it is supported and refined by meditation that knowledge is fruitful and blessed, it is only when it is supported and refined by such knowledge that the spirit can become free".

Is that an accurate translation, Martin?'

'Yes, that's it.'

'And where did you come across this particular formulation?'

'This is a translation by Professor Hermann Beckh who was a Sanscrit scholar and in my opinion a very great one, who then translated the writings of the Buddha in a most beautiful and poetic way. You'll find this passage in his book *Der Hingang des*

Vollendeten.' [1]

'I'm not acquainted with the statement, testament, in that form.'

'It is to me one of the profoundest and clearest statements ever made on the spiritual life, and Professor Beckh, who later became a priest in the Christian Community, based his book *Buddha und seine Lehre* — which I think is one of the most remarkable ever written on the Buddha, with the profoundest understanding of the master and his teaching — just on this formula. Now, if you approach it with, if you like, an analytical — a mildly analytical! — attitude you can see that four stages are mentioned, namely, first, the *sittliche Selbsterziehung,* or, as we put it in a previous conversation, a character training. It is really training of the whole personality, it is not only the training of your thought, but of your emotions, your feelings, your will, your attitude to life altogether.'

'A life of personal discipline?'

'Yes, a life of personal discipline, life in relation to others, and so on. It goes into the smallest details of personal conduct, for instance, even into the details of how you should move, how you should speak, how you should be silent, how you should sit down, get up, even how you should perform your bodily functions, you see. It is a kind of enlightened awareness of everything you do, without, of course, the overtones and stresses of self-consciousness. It is the total co-ordination of the human being and the co-ordination of his relationship to the world.'

'Body, spirit and relationships?', I ventured to interpose.

'Exactly, everything. Now this is No. 1, and of course this is extremely far-reaching and will permeate and penetrate the whole of your day. You can then speak, as very many spiritual techers have also spoken, about — I say it again first in German: *'Der Alltag als Uebung':* everyday life itself becomes an area of exercise and moral training for you. And he says that without this meditation cannot be, as he says, *ertragreich,* fruitful, productive, and *segensvoll,* beneficial, full of blessing, because it needs the well-structured foundation of discipline and control.'

'The soil?'

'Yes, the soil', Dr. Gregory continued, 'in order to approach, to enter into the sphere of thought, or pondering. He calls it *Sinnen,* a very beautiful word. You need this character-training in order to maintain yourself in this sphere of thought and pondering, without

61

being thrown into chaos, fantasising, or whatever it may be, holding fast to the same clarity, the same control there as you have in ordinary life.

So we go from *moralische Selbsterziehung* or character training into the sphere of meditation. This is realm two. As we enter more and more deeply into such a way of life, it is the general experience that we enter into the realm of meditation — and I say "general experience" advisedly because we are here not discussing primarily Buddhist meditation. That would be a wrong assumption. No, the Buddhist way is simply one classical, though almost pre-eminent, form of the archetypal spiritual path which, as such, is present in one or other form in all classical traditions of the spiritual path, including the Hindu one, and also the Western one. It is only a matter of difference of terminology.'

'It is a particular way of expressing a universal possibility of experience, with universal stages?'.

'Quite, and the universal stages are these four. So we come to meditation. What happens is that you penetrate more and more deeply into the discipline of your way of life and then into the content of your meditation, and this may be greatly varied. It is very varied for me: it may be a sentence or a scene from the New Testament, primarily St John's gospel, because that is the gospel of the Word, or it may be something out of the *Bhagavad Gita*, or it may be something out of the discourses of the Buddha, or even a great poem. The less sensory content it has, the better, of course, the more it'll help you to become liberated from your body and from your intellect. And as you thus become more and more liberated from the body and the intellect and penetrate more and more deeply into what you are meditating, the border-line between you and the object of your meditation begins to dwindle, it begins to vanish away, you become submerged in it. And what usually happens (not by all means all the time) is that in the end your mind begins to rest, focus, on one word, — say, the word "holiness" or "joy", or whatever it may be, while the other words, as you more and more relinquish rational consciousness, begin to, you might say, melt away, dissolve. So you focus in the end on this one concentrated word. And then even this begins to melt away and becomes a kind of atmosphere, and only an awareness of this word remains. Can you imagine what I mean?'

'And this is stage three', I asked.

'We are now approaching stage three, yes.'

'What does the Buddha call that?'

'Stage three he calls *Erkenntnis,* intuitive knowledge, yes? Now we have reached a stage where the rational discursive consciousness has faded away, and only the essence, as it were, the awareness, if you like the *taste* of what you have meditated on, has remained.'

'I think that this is what St Thomas Aquinas called the *simplex intuitus veritatis,* the simple intuition of the truth.'

'Yes, now we come to that. And at this stage, you have to be able to hold your mind completely still or to do what Jakob Böhme said you have to do when he was asked, "How can I experience God?" namely, "Put yourself out of the way". And this applies particularly here. Then, to the extent that you can do this very difficult thing of putting yourself completely out of the way, then you will enter this next stage, however slightly, and have the experience of intuitive knowledge. Now the great question is what is meant by intuitive knowledge?'

'This is now realm three?' I asked again.

'This is realm three, *Erkenntnis.* For the Buddha this was perfectly clear: he perceived very clearly his own former lives; he was able to follow the destiny of beings as they go through the cycle of rebirth; he described super-sensible beings and found the great truth concerning suffering and the overcoming of suffering; super-sensible powers of hearing and seeing enabled him to know what was far beyond ordinary human perception and knowledge. In this way the super-sensible world opened up for him. Now I think that for ordinary mortals it is as if one were standing on a beach, and one felt — not saw — perhaps very faintly, one felt and heard, slightly, the sound of the waves surging towards one, and one knew that one was standing on the border-line of a different world. And what this different world conveys to you is simply that there is something beyond the material which very, very gently and slightly begins to speak to you; it begins to *sound* to you and it begins to *light* up for you, and it has *being* and it has *movement.* There is one specially wonderful expression of this and one word in particular which I've loved for a long time, in Thomas à Kempis. Characteristically his *Imitation of Christ* is also in four parts, and with the passage I have in mind we are at the beginning of Part III, so we're standing again at exactly the same point we've reached in our present discussion. And what Thomas à Kempis says — I'll read it first in German again, then translate it into English — is:

"*Lass mich horen* — Let me hear": listening — "*was in mir Gott redet* — what God is saying within me": so you begin to hear. Now: "*Selige Ohren die das Nahen des göttlichen Rauschens vernehmen, und von den Geräuschen dieser Welt nichts innewerden* — "Blessed are the ears which take in the sounding of God as he approaches and which perceive nothing of the noise of this world."

Now this "*göttliche Rauschen*" — we may say the gentle sounding, murmuring, of a super-sensible world — seems to be wonderfully expressed, and in so-called spontaneous, *super-sensible*, mystical experiences, this particular fact of the experience of *sound* is very often emphasised. The translation I've got goes like this: "Blessed are the ears that catch the breath of the whisper of God." That's beautiful, isn't it? "And give no heed to the whispering of this world."

Now this is one characteristic aspect of such an experience: the fact that you hear something that strikes you as the manifestation of something which is beyond the natural world. But you can also experience it in the form of certain more clearly defined sounds, which therefore seem to be inspired sounds, in which case you have music; or you can experience such sounding in the form of more definite words, which seem to be equally inspired, in which case you have poetry. And therefore this world has also been called the world of inspiration.'

'It's the world of what have been called the *Urworte*, the primordial sounds, of the sounds before they articulate themselves in particular ways, into the great poetry of the world, or the Scriptures — primordial sound?'

'Exactly. It has also been called the *Weltensprache*, I mean the archetypal sound-language of the world. Now the great poet, in a moment of inspiration, or the great musician, like Mozart, is entered into by this world, or enters into this world, you see. And therefore these geniuses, like Mozart, were always experienced as people who didn't belong to the earth but lived on a different level of consciousness — unconsciously, of course. This, then, is what the Buddha means by *Erkenntnis*. Again I repeat, whilst his

Erkenntnis, his knowledge was of course exceedingly clear and definite, what we ordinary mortals can expect is an awareness, an *Erkenntnis,* an intuition, in various ways, of a world which is beyond the material world, and perhaps occasionally more. Right? So we can enter the fourth stage. Now we must have the strength even to leave this world behind and enter — this is particularly difficult, the most difficult part of it — the world of complete stillness, where our being and our own perceptions, even what we have discerned at stage three, are so subdued that we are ready to encounter something that is ultimately beyond words and beyond description. It has the character of "mystical silence" (*silentium mysticum*) and through it we may experience something like an encounter with "a presence" which may or may not reveal its nature. What one encounters at this level one can't describe, because the moment one begins to describe it, one falsifies its nature. It is beyond description, it is beyond discursive explanation. It is an encounter with something which you feel utterly and which in every way transcends your ordinary comprehension, and yet you experience it as a reality.'

'It sounds to me rather like what St Ignatius of Antioch, at the end of the first century A.D., called the mystery of silence — the mystery of silence that cries out for expression. So behind the primordial sound that lies behind articulate speech is the primordial silence?'

'Yes, that is very well put: it's a primordial silence, and it is this, as far as one can put it in human terms, which, I think, the human heart and the human spirit longs to achieve, namely, stillness. You learn to surmount the various areas of, well, unrest, stress and almost disintegration, until you come to a sphere where you can rest in complete silence, in complete stillness, whatever it may be.'

'By passing over these various thresholds?'

'Yes, by passing over these various thresholds. And the mystics have described all this in various ways. Of course, it depends largely on the individual personality.'

'And culture?'

'And culture. I believe that Aquinas described it as an almost death-like stage: you have died into something higher, and died certainly to yourself and to the world. In this connection, I often recall an expression of Rilke, who was, of course, very aware of the tragic nature of the human condition. He spoke of men as *"wir, die Zerfallenden,* we who disintegrate". In everything and at every moment we are in danger of distintegrating, in our thoughts, in our feelings, in our very bodies, but the moment we have achieved the crossing of the various thresholds into what you call so well primordial silence, then disintegration is behind us.'

'Well, if I may come in here, Martin, I'd like to say that this is wholly illuminating, and from very many points of view. Because we've spoken about the subject quite a number of times, directly or indirectly, and I know that it's something very dear to your heart. But what is new to me is your starting from this quotation from the Buddha. I don't remember your ever having done so before with me. And I dare say that you've chosen it because it expresses with unexampled succinctness the essential content but also the, as you say, structure, the dynamics, if you like, of the spiritual life, the stages of the spiritual path, which can be schematically and analytically divided into these four: the character training, the meditation, this intuitive awareness, and then finally the...'

'liberation'

'liberation into a meeting, into a sense of the transcendent *other* of some sort, is that right? Now one of the reasons why I find this very enriching is because, when you have spoken about this subject before, you've done it in terms of the more Western tradition and the corresponding scheme of the *via purgativa,* the *via illumimativa* and the *via unitiva.* We have already agreed this morning that the value of this particular statement of the Buddha is that it is particular in expression but universal in scope. So it's not surprising to find the essential content re-expressed in different terms, in different traditions, in different cultures. But I wonder whether you would like to say a bit more about its re-expression in this Western mode, Martin?'

'Yes. Well, first of all, I particularly like your word "dynamism", because I think that the whole discussion of the spiritual path should be based on the fact and the acceptance of the fact that it is something which is the spiritual equivalent of an organic dynamism. Just as there is an organic necessity to pass through certain stages, for example, in the assimilation of food (chewing, digesting, resorption or whatever), or certain stages of muscular activity in order to move and to climb, so we also have to move as it were organically along the spiritual path, in these four stages, if we take it really seriously and are determined to reach our goal. Then we are simply being carried from one stage into the next — provided we have the staying power. Therefore, you see, it is perfectly inevitable that though the terminology may change, the actual dynamics will never change. And if they do change, it is a sign that arbitrariness and illusion are creeping in. Therefore I firmly believe that if we want the truth about it, we must keep to the archetypal or classical tradition.'

'Because it is founded on human nature?'

'Because it is founded on human nature, and something you can change as little as you can change the fact that you have to breathe in and out if you want to breathe normally.'

'Or that normally you pass through certain developmental stages as part of becoming more and more fully human?', I asked.

'Exactly, through youth, middle age, life generally.'

'And that each stage is divided by what the anthropologists might call a *rite de passage*, a rite of passage — precisely a death and a rebirth into the next stage?'

'Yes, I think that is it particularly important to realise this, because there is a danger and also a certain temptation of, to put it very naively, getting stuck at certain stages. And it requires great effort, concentration and awareness to go beyond that stage, and particularly, as I mentioned, to enter ultimately into that primordial silence.'

'Again I suppose that this is the equivalent of what the psycho-analysts would call "being fixated", so that the whole business of therapy, especially psycho-analytic therapy, is to release people from being "fixated", from being stuck, in order that they can resume the spontaneous dynamic growth that belongs to them as human beings. That's what you're saying?'

'Exactly, that's what I'm saying. You see, it is in this respect also highly characteristic and significant that it is called a *path:* a path is there to walk along, and you may imagine it as a mountain path which leads upwards.

Then, as far as the comparison of the Western and Eastern traditions is concerned, I see no difficulty here at all. Quite clearly the *via purgativa* is the equivalent of the character training, it is the purifying of your ordinary human nature, isn't it? Then, as far as I know, in the Western tradition, the words meditation and contemplation also enter, don't they? Now if we move on through meditation to contemplation, then contemplation designates the fact and the stage when ordinary discursive consciousness begins to fade away and you are on the threshold of something else, having left behind the discursive consciousness of what is technically stage two.'

'Can I just pause there, Martin', I interjected, 'because I now see the solution to a difficulty I've had whenever you've talked about the Western way of articulating the spiritual path. For, on the one hand, you have faithfully reported the Western tradition to say that there are *three* aspects or parts of the spiritual life: the *via purgativa*, the *via illuminativa* and the *via unitiva* — three, whereas on other occasions, on the other hand, you have talked, as you have again talked today, of *four* stages. Now, in view of what you have just said, we can resolve this little intellectual puzzle by saying that the three Western *viae* or ways express the successively dominant characteristics of the experience of the growing spiritual life rather than the successive stages of awareness but that they do correspond to modes of prayer and therefore to stages of awareness, and that as such the *via illuminativa* can be sub-divided to include *both* the stage of meditation *and* the stage of contemplation. Therefore the stage of meditation in the Western sense corresponds to the Buddha's meditation, whereas contemplation in the Western sense would then, presumably, correspond to his *Erkenntnis*, intuitive knowledge?'

'Well, I've experienced it differently', responded Dr. Gregory.

'Ah', I said.

'You seen, the very word "illumination" indicates that you are, well, suddenly illumined, that you see something, and to me this is an experience which very much belongs to the sphere of stage three, to intuitive knowledge, where you suddenly see the truth, literally see something which you haven't so far seen, in a spontaneously arising image or symbol. And contemplation, or meditation, represent stages of approach, steps of approach to the state of illumination which I believe is identical with stage three, the stage of *Erkenntnis*, of intuitive knowledge.'

'This may be just a question of words. I think I should tend to think of contemplation in the sense in which St Thomas talks about it — in terms of *simplex intuitus veritatis*. For him simple intuition (and he deliberately uses the word *intuitus*, intuition, not *ratio*, the discursive activity of the mind, as I've indicated to you before) is the essence of contemplation, and then I think it would be the equivalent of your illumination, not merely an approach to it.'

'Absolutely, yes. You see, it's very difficult to equate the terminology exactly because different people and different teachers have attached slightly varying meanings to different terms. So I don't think there is really any difficulty at all. Quite clearly, of course, what in the Buddha's terminology is called liberation, or what you call entering into the primordial silence and into the other being, is the *unio mystica*. So it is exactly the same path, it is bound to be the same path. And when you read — I read this book quite a bit and although it is too large and over-written, it is a classic of its kind — Evelyn Underhill's *Mysticism*, you see that a quite amazing amount of super-sensible knowledge has entered the minds of the mystics on the way to the *unio mystica*, which is the ultimate aim. So it is one and the same path. There is another book which I much appreciate and which has come out fairly recently. Admittedly it concentrates primarily on the Eastern tradition, but by no means only, and it is called *The Variety of Meditative Experience*, obviously deriving its title from William James' *The Variety of Religious Experience*. And the essential message of the book is again that, although the *terminology* differs, the basic *dynamics* are the same.'

'Well, as I say, what is new for me in today's discussion, Martin, is your placing the topic of the spiritual path within the context of that peculiarly condensed saying of the Buddha. I can also see that it has been present to you for a long time but I haven't been aware of it being so explicitly part of your learning and life. Then there's one other thing I'd like to hear you commenting on. In all this exposition, you've spoken primarily in terms of knowledge, and only once, I think, have you used the term "heart" which I take to stand for the more affective side. And as I understand the subject of prayer and meditation in the Western tradition, prayer is essentially a matter ultimately of the *heart*. If you take a classical formulation of the tradition such as that of St Francis de Sales in his instructions to beginners on how to pray, you'll find he is very concerned about the preparation — not only the remote preparation of daily life, as you interpreted the Buddha to be saying, but also the more immediate preparation of putting yourself in the presence of God, of the use of the imagination (what St Ignatius of Loyola calls the "composition of place") of the gradual stilling of the powers of the body and the interior powers of the imagination, and even of the intellect, the reason. And for him all this preparation is in the interest of, and is directed towards what I call the *kindling of the heart*. You see that, whether or not prayer ultimately grows — is given to grow — into the higher reaches of illumination or even union, it is essentially a matter of the heart.'

'Yes. Can I say something to that?' Dr. Gregory asked.

'Yes.'

'Well, the first thing is by way of a personal remark: that through my destiny, or, perhaps, through my constitutionally more contemplative disposition, I was more drawn to and also taught about meditation than about prayer in the spiritual path. But I believe that apart from my contemplative inclination, I am essentially a feeling person. Apart from these personal remarks, however, I should say that if you want to enter a meditative content, your essential guide, the essential force which you use, is feeling. The moment you begin to use intellect, you are lost because you dissociate yourself from the content of your meditation. So from the word go, you must immerse yourself through your feelings in what you meditate. You must attend, for instance, not so much to what the words mean but to how they sound, and if they don't touch your heart and your feelings, you will get nowhere. And this of course permeates the whole way upwards. This is number one. Number two, equally important, and perhaps even more so, is that when you encounter this presence, this otherness, which you may do at the end of the path, it will not just remain there but it will enter you. It will begin to permeate you, and Ignatius of Loyola, and other people too, used a very wonderful comparison, namely, eating. It is something which you can drink, or which wants to be drunk and to be eaten by you. It simply begins to descend into you. That is the experience. You see right away the relationship with communion. It is, spiritually speaking, communion. And here, of course, the most important phase of this feeding, of this nourishment, is that it fills and nourishes the heart and gives you in this sphere nourishment and strength.'

'So you would agree that at every stage it is the heart which is primary?'

'Absolutely'

'That the training is essentially a training of the heart, of the feelings, of the affectivity; that the meditation, even the contemplation, is with a view to the stilling of the heart; that the higher stage, the listening, is a listening with the heart?'

'Exactly'

'And that the *unio,* if it is given to one, any union, of any quality, of any explicitness, is a union, as it has been said, of the heart to the heart, *cor ad cor?* You'd agree with that?'

'Absolutely. It's again, of course, not for nothing that Buddha's teaching has been called *"die Lehre von Liebe und Mitleid* — the teaching about love and compassion." I don't need to tell you anything about the Christian concept of any meditation. But perhaps it's a good moment, if you like, to remind ourselves of that lovely summary which I've quoted to you before.'

'The one about the *Umarmung,* the embrace, you mean?'.

'Yes, may I read it out to you in its entirety, because it depicts this element of sublime love and union so beautifully. It comes from the *Upanishads.* Again I'll read it in the German translation where I discovered it:

So wie ein Mann in der innigsten Umarmung seines geliebten Weibes von nichts mehr weiss, weder von Aeusserem noch von Innerem, so geht es diesem Menschen; in innigsten Umarmung des erkennenden Selbst (Atman) *weiss er nichts mehr, weder von Aeusserem noch von Innerem. Das ist der Seinszustand, wo er der Sorgen ledig, wo sein Sehnen erfüllt ist, wo sein einziger Wunsch das Selbst* (Atman) *ist, und in sich hat er keine Wünsche mehr, die Welt keine Welt mehr, sind die Götter keine Götter mehr...ein Asket kein Asket mehr. Nicht mehr achtend der guten Werke, nicht mehr achtend der bösen Werke, ist er hinübergelangt ans andere Ufer und er hat die Kümmernisse des Herzens hinter sich gelassen.[2] (translated in footnote below)*

*The translation of this passage contained in R.C. Zaehner *Hindu Scriptures* (pp 67-8, Everyman Library, London, 1966) goes as follows:
21. 'Just as a man, closely embraced by his loving wife, knows nothing

So, you see, even here we have the element of surrendering and giving love, of the highest order.'

'I think that's peculiarly beautiful, and very relevant to the whole series of discussions, because not only does it sum up the inner dynamic of the path we've been talking about this morning, that thrust or élan towards union which, therefore, when it is achieved, as it were dissolves all the forms of separation there are — between the ego and the greater self, between inner and outer, between the self and the other: that is the mystery, the ultimately ineffable mystery of the *unio mystica* — but it makes the transition to the heart again, as we were just saying; it emphasises the heart, the warmth of love rather than the light of knowledge. But even more than that, I think, what is so fascinating is that it does so in terms of the basic human experience of the love of man and woman. At the same time, it transforms that. It expresses itself in terms of that basic experience but it takes it into a higher realm, and so it really draws together practically all the themes we have talked about in this series: the theme of being with another, the real quality and meaning of the depths of such an experience; the experience of solitude as distinct from loneliness; the relationship between a man and a woman; and all this it seems to subsume and draw upwards in this beautiful expression about the *innigste Umarmung*, the innermost embrace.'

'Exactly', said Dr. Gregory.

'Very beautiful indeed'.

'One might say, in a very banal way, this is really what life is all about. If there is any answer to man's predicament and to the multitude of predicaments, then the answer's there'.

'It's a question once again of allowing the implications and depths of ordinary life and ordinary encounters to be touched and explored and followed through with persistence — and ardour, very

without, nothing within, so does this "person", closely embraced by the Self that consists of wisdom (*prājña*) know nothing without, nothing within. That is his [true] form in which [all] his desires are fulfilled, in which Self [alone] is his desire, in which he has no desire, no sorrow.
22. These....states of being (*loka*) are no longer states of being, gods are no longer gods....an ascetic no longer an ascetic. He is not followed by good, not followed by evil; for then he will have passed beyond all sorrow of the heart.'[2]

great ardour, what the Hindus call *tapas,* energy, fiery energy.'

'The ardour: I'm glad you mention that, because anything lukewarm will not do. This is perhaps again a matter of training and habit in the best sense of the word, the habit that becomes part of you, second nature. So that in the end you pursue this path with the ardour, the longing of a lover, in the highest sense of this word. If you haven't got that, you will not get there. Certainly not with the interest simply of somebody who wants to know.'

'And perhaps with that word "lover" we are once again at the full, the glowing centre of all the traditions: the tradition of the *Symposium* and of Plato in the West, the tradition of the *Bhagavad Gita* in the East, and so on. I should like to say that here we are at the glowing centre, the burning core, not so much of the material world, not even of the spiritual world, but of the world that is patient of being spiritualised, the one *cosmos.*'

'Yes, indeed', said Dr. Gregory, and so closed this morning's discussion.

notes

1. Verlag Urachhaus, Stuttgart, 2nd Edn., 1960.

2. *Brihadāranyaka Upanishad,* 4,3. 21-22, quoted in Udo Reiter *Meditation-Wege zum Selbst* (Mosaik Verlag, Munich, 1976 p.47).

It could be noted that Zaehner translates the text in terms of a man *being* embraced by his wife and then by the Self, whereas the translator into German translates his text in terms of what could be taken as *his* embrac*ing* his wife and then the knowing Self — a difference between passive and active from the man's point of view. Now apart from the uncertainity as to whether the genitive in the German translation is subjective or objective, and apart from the question of the text translated by Reiter and Zaehner respectively, two interesting problems lie behind these technicalities. Even if the English translation envisages the individual subject *being* embraced and the German envisages him embracing, the very complementarity of the translations brings out something which the perhaps deliberate ambiguity of the German also brings out in any case, namely, that there is a *mutual* embrace or implication and therefore a unification between the individual mortal and the divine principle. At the same time this very complementarity, as well as the contrast between the persistence of the two subjects of the unification and the unification intended, both nicely leave open the large philosophical question whether the unification involved is to be understood in terms of what Radhakrishnan has called pure or modified monism (*Indian Philosophy,* London, George Allen and Unwin, 2nd Edn., 1929, I, pp.31-34). For, as has been very acutely observed, there can be non-dualism without monism, so that the undoubted principle of *Advaita,* a-dualism, is open to two very different interpretations: in terms of the dissolution of one principle into the other, like the proverbial drop in the ocean or the camphor in the flame, or in terms of the abiding co-existence of both man and God. The critical question is whether those who were formerly two attain a union of fusion or a union in distinction. The latter is, I believe, the fundamental Christian position, but is it also the Hindu position? Is it one possible interpretation of the Hindu position, or is it excluded by it? See on this subject Michael Simpson 'Hinduism and Christianity' in *The Tablet* 30th August 1980, pp.842-3

dialogue 6: stages of counselling in relation to stages of the spiritual path

'I'm very glad that you've come to keep our usual appointment, Marcus', began Dr. Martin this particular morning, 'even though you've got a touch of laryngitis. I'm sorry about your indisposition, but I'd like — if I may say so without appearing to be unfeeling — to take advantage of your relative voicelessness to tell you about a certain experience I had recently when I was working with a client. For this experience has a bearing on two of the major topics we've discussed together so far, namely, the stages of counselling and the stages of the spiritual path, in so far as it revealed to me something of the relationship of the spiritual life to the actual event of counselling.

Now you will recall that in a previous conversation, we defined the four basic stages of the spiritual path, namely, first, a moral training or the *via purgativa*, a character training, as I called it; secondly, the stage of meditation, which then proceeds into the third stage of contemplation or illumination or intuitive knowledge, the stage at which we transcend thinking and perceive truth intuitively; and, fourthly, the stage of liberation, of union, where we are able to enter something which is completely beyond our ordinary self. This may be our own higher self, it may be something of a divine nature, or, in ordinary life, the very existence of another being with whom we then become intuitively identified.

So far, and in this way, then, we have been thinking about the spiritual path as a path of human development and purification, as a way of transcending our lower self, of transformation and perfection. However, the experience which I want to describe to you today adds a completely new dimension to this matter. For what I learned in it was that if we are living constantly in the dynamic, so to speak, of this life and proceeding through these stages, if we are walking foward and upward on this path, then, even in ordinary life, and particularly in the counselling situation, we will, in relation to our clients, develop certain perceptions which would otherwise be denied to us, at least in the same way. I mean that perceptions which I believe are extremely important and helpful would not occur to us in the same way.

This is a bald statement of my discovery, but to put you in the picture, I'd like to take a few steps back and say that I had to prepare for a counselling session with someone who is a friend of mine. He had come from a foreign country and I knew in advance that he had led a life which was very disappointing to me. He had developed relationships, multiple relationships, to women, among them to the wife of his best friend. He had rather lost his way and got involved in a number of very questionable intellectual and spiritual activities. I therefore approached this encounter with considerable apprehension, and I knew that I could function properly only if I were able to overcome this apprehension or any possible resentment or disappointment I might feel. It therefore needed a more than usually intense effort of preparation to get ready for this session. Now you know my idea of preparing by achieving a state of inner stillness or what I have in another context called a state of innocence, in which one frees oneself as far as is possible from all prejudices, personal preoccupations, thoughts and feelings, and achieves a state of inner stillness which can perhaps best be likened to the stillness of a lake on a windless sunny day: you can look through the surface of the lake right into the clear depths whilst clouds that glide through the sky are mirrored in the surface. That is, of course, a poetic image, a classical image, and I make no claims to have achieved this stillness completely, but on this occasion I tried to be completely calm and I think that I did to some extent achieve that state. Now, quite clearly, this is the stage that corresponds to the first stage of the spiritual life, the stage of character training or *via purgativa*.

The next thing was that I became aware that I was listening in a kind of meditative attitude. I'm sure I had done this before but now

I was simply more conscious of doing so. Now what does it mean to listen in a meditative attitude? I think it means that you subdue your intellect, you make this effort of subduing your conscious intellectual mind which works by searching for sharply defined impressions and looking for signs and symptoms, which is constantly aware in terms of concepts, which is inclined right away to draw conclusions and to make judgments and so on. It's all this that needs to be subdued. I'm not suggesting that all this work should completely vanish from your mind, because here and there you will probably have to use your conscious mind. But, generally speaking, in order to open yourself up to taking in the full reality of what comes towards you as an experience, you will have to do that. I could put it like this: to vary a phrase of Rudolf Steiner I have previously quoted to you, namely, 'You must learn to think whilst abstaining from thinking', you must here learn to listen whilst abstaining from thinking, and then the inner state of being in the person whom you meet will gradually begin to light up. Images — characteristic images, significant images — will begin to develop, begin to become more intense and will as it were come towards you. You will not search for them; they will come towards you and will eventually impress themselves on your mind — they may be images strictly so called, or certain words certain gestures. As you listen and observe, you will have an experience comparable with the experience of observing colours and shapes, of listening to sounds and tunes, and also comparable with experiencing objects and the world of objects through the senses of touch, taste, even of smell. So that when you have fully absorbed or taken in such an experience, you are filled not only in the intellectual sense — that perhaps least of all — but by way of a *soul-experience,* which penetrates right into your very organism. You have taken it in, in the same way as you take in something when you eat and drink; you have drunk it in, you have to some extent allowed yourself to drink it in, in a restrained way. The experience, will, therefore, have a palpable reality which you will not be able to question — as little as you question the experience of being out in nature and seeing trees, stones, smelling the air, experiencing the sunshine.

Now this experience of immersing yourself, being filled with impressions of that kind has an obvious affinity with the activity of meditation. Therefore I think it is justifiable to call it an attitude of *meditative listening* and observing. And the more you have schooled yourself in meditation, where it is fundamental not only to subdue your intellect and the activities of your brain but to transcend them, the easier you will find it to listen and observe in this attitude.

The next stage of the spiritual path, as you know, is the stage of so-called illumination or intuitive knowledge. And it was after I had thoroughly immersed myself in the personality, presentation and problems of my friend in this attitude of meditative listening that I became particularly conscious that something so to speak *happened* to me which I had not experienced with such intensity before. After I had heard the experiences which this person, my friend, related to me — and it was a very complex story, and a story of many conflicts — he asked me a question, for he had to make a decision. Now what I experienced was that I did not have to think about it but could immediately give him an answer which I instinctively felt to be the right one. It offered itself to me, so to speak, as naturally as breathing does. I'm not saying, and I don't want to say, that this was a particularly difficult question. I'm quite sure that I or any other person would have been able to answer this question after giving it a little thought. But what I do want to say — this was the experience that alerted me — is that in actual fact I didn't think at all about it consciously. The answer presented itself convincingly to me and with equal conviction to the other person. At that moment I experienced a transition from the stage of meditative listening and observing to something akin to and comparable with intuitive knowledge.

Then, however, the experience went even further, and I felt, as our session continued, that my thoughts about his conflict situation and the answer I had given, as well as all the experiences which he had related to me, began as it were to vanish. More and more I felt *him* and his state of being as he was. I felt so to speak identified with him in a — perhaps this is the right word — existential way. I suddenly knew what it was and how it was to be him at that moment. There were no thoughts about him. The whole conflict and all the experiences had dissolved but I felt him. And the feeling I had was of being stressed and strained, so to speak, in various ways, with forces pulling powerfully from the periphery in various directions, and of the centre more and more weakening. And I believe that essentially this was his problem: that he had lost contact with his centre, his essential inner self which had begun so to speak to weaken or perhaps even to disintegrate. Now I believe that this experience of identification is nothing but an equivalent of the experience of union, the last stage in the spiritual life where the person identifies with, enters into, something which is not himself but another being, another reality which he begins now to know and more than know, to identify with, to slip into, as it were from within.

I think that these few remarks will make it sufficiently clear that the spiritual life is not only a great training ·ground for the purification and development of one's own personality but also the training ground for enabling one to have certain perceptions during the counselling session and to relate to a client in a way which would otherwise not be possible, at least with the same clarity, certainty, the same insight. Anybody who begins to think about it will, I believe, readily be able to relate the so-called seven stages of the counselling process to the four stages of the path. They interlink, and as the counselling process continues, so the developing stages of consciousness of the path help one to understand and move the counselling process forward again, as in a spiral. They are in fact interacting constantly. We become aware of this, and if we live the counselling encounter through in this way, then we realise that the counselling process and the stages of the path are one interlinked, integrated whole. They belong together — perhaps this is an adequate comparison — as breathing and the heart-beat belong together.

In conclusion I should like to say that just as the counselling process in its various stages manifests the archetype of the *Gespräch*, the dialogue, so the spiritual life as I have now discussed it can manifest and does manifest in real life the archetype of true relatedness and deeper mutual understanding.'

'Well, Martin', I said, when we were able to meet again the next time, 'I think that your new insight is indeed something of a breakthrough. I'm captivated by it, and in a way I'm glad that I could not speak last time since you were as a result able to express your thought in a single flow. But now that I am able to respond and, in addition, have had time to think over what you said the last time, I should like to say that you've aroused my critical as well as my creative spirit. You've enabled me to glimpse certain connections I've never glimpsed before. But I'd like to deal first with what I call the critical part of my reflections. So may I say that, stimulating as your most recent thinking is, it does pose something of an intellectual problem for me, in so far as I do *not* see exactly how the seven stages of the counselling process relate to, fit in with, the four stages of the spiritual development. I realise that you did suggest something of the way these respective stages matched up with each other, but I must admit that at least to my — over? — logical mind this correlation seemed to be at once too vague and too forced.'

'Well', rejoined Dr. Gregory, 'let me try to meet your query — though you realise that this sort of more exact thinking is not really my line! Starting, then, with the first stage of the counselling process, the stage of preparation, this is a matter of clearing one's mind of all intruding thoughts, feelings, conceptions, which presupposes a training in character that is the subject-matter of the first stage of the spiritual life. The second stage of counselling is the state of listening, primarily of listening but also, of course, to some extent, of exploring. And here the meditative attitude which I have described in relation to the second stage of the spiritual life comes into play, although occasionally it may be interrupted by a very conscious attempt to question and to explore. So we come to the third stage of counselling, the stage of assimilation, of inwardly absorbing what we have heard, and this is even more markedly correlated with the meditative attitude. (And I should like to remind you that the stage of assimilation and the stage of the diagnostic interlude are inter-changeable).

From there we move on the to next stage, the fourth, the stage of the diagnostic interlude. Quite clearly this has something to do with the act of knowing. We must consciously make a diagnosis, but we all know that the diagnosis can be a very, very subtle matter and even for the most professional mind it is often overlaid with a great deal of uncertainty. Even at the strictly psychological level, many psychiatrists, for example, will in all sincerity make very different diagnoses. Besides which, I personally, as you know, try to take into account a person's physical constitution and cosmological position as well as his biography and development. In all these circumstances, therefore, our intuitive knowledge will be a most valuable guide in sorting out our uncertainties in this sphere, helping us to make the right diagnosis.

So we proceed to stage five in the sequence of counselling, the selection of the target area. Again this to some extent must be a conscious act but it is ultimately as subtle as, or even more subtle than, becoming clear about the diagnosis. And once again our intuitive feelings, our intuitive knowledge, that which arises from within with a sense of certainty apart from and beyond any conscious thought, will be a precious instrument. Therefore this is again related to the area of intuitive knowledge.

The next stage again, stage six, consists in working through the target area with the client. Quite obviously this is already in a much more marked degree than at the previous stages a matter of the relationship of the therapist to the client. He must guide him, and the more clearly he feels what kind of person the client is — feels his very being, the more he feels identified with him — the more certainty he will have, the more assurance he will have to guide him. At this stage, therefore, we have what I believe is a significant transition from the realm of intuitive knowledge to the realm of identification. And this pertains even more to the last stage, stage seven of the counselling process, when the client has lived through the essential stages and phases of the therapeutic process and has now reached the point of adjusting to life, of finding a foothold in life again, of discovering new insights, new attitudes, new values, which will help him to start again. Here, quite clearly, the more we shall have exercised our capacity to identify with him, to feel him as he is, beyond all thoughts and concepts, the more we will be able to guide, to help, to support.

So, you see, that is the way I see the two schemes — of the counselling process and of the spiritual life — fitting together. Is that clearer? But let me just add this, I've again spoken about a scheme. I do, however, want to insist that ultimately this is abstract, whereas the whole process of counselling is a living process in a constant flux. Nothing is fixed, and if an abstract scheme such as I have outlined intrudes, and particularly if it intrudes permanently, it drives the very life out of this living encounter between two human beings. Any scheme — this one included — is nothing but the bare, dry bones, it *is* a structure, and this structure must sink into the very depths of our being, where it belongs, just to give us a kind of foundation, a kind of supportive foundation on which the edifice of the creative action must be built. You can therefore compare it with the scheme and structure which a creative musician has to learn when he learns the technique of composition. If he *is* a creative artist, all this will sink into the very depths of his being, and from there it will allow the creation of a work of art. It is basically exactly the same in counselling: we need the structure in order to have the foundation, because we are always in danger of losing shape in our thoughts, in our approach, in our attitude, in our whole being. As I've mentioned already, Rilke once spoke of men as *die Zerfallenden,* those liable to fall apart. We can indeed slowly, imperceptibly disintegrate, and the structure, once it is acquired and deeply sunk into the foundation of our being, will help us not to disintegrate. But, apart from that, the encounter must be an act of creation, adjusted to the uniqueness of the situation and to the uniqueness of the individual. So what we must realise above all is that in such an encounter we are creating something, and creating something out of what is in flux, as life in the cosmos is in flux. I think yet once again of Goethe's lines:

> *Gestaltung, Umgestaltung*
> *Des ewigen Sinnes ewige Unterhaltung.*

For Goethe life is a matter of the forming and unforming of some eternal meaning that eternally sustains us. And, with that caution, do you understand how in my thinking the two "schemes" fit together?'

'With my feeling and intuitive being, Martin', I replied, 'I find all this wholly fascinating and real, and yet, with my critical being, I must admit to still having certain doubts. My thoughts are still a little too turbulent at the moment for me quite to be able to work them through, but, trying to frame them as best I can, I feel, on the one hand, that in the reformulation of your case to meet my query you were not quite true to your own initial intuition, but that, on the other hand, you are saying something extremely valuable which could be reformulated and, in the reformulation, be seen to be something different from and, *therefore,* also something even more profound than you seem to be saying immediately.'

'Possibly', said Dr. Gregory, a little doubtfully.

'You see, Martin, to take the negative part of my response to you first, I think that my question about the exact manner of interrelation between the stages of counselling and the stages of spiritual development and its accompanying degrees of consciousness go to the heart of your thesis *as* you propound it. What I want to say about this inter-relationship is parallel to what I said about the previous inter-relationship you sought to establish between the stages of counselling and the stages of an ordinary but true dialogue, a *Gespräch*, between friends who as such enjoy equality. Do you remember how, when I sought to test whether there was a point-by-point correlation between the two sorts of exchange, we got a bit unstuck? You had to labour to establish a point-by-point correspondence then, didn't you, just as in my opinion you had to labour just now to establish the details of the correlation between the stages of counselling and the stages of the spiritual life.'

'Yes. Can I interrupt you for a moment?', asked Dr. Gregory.

'Of course', I replied.

'It's exactly as you say. Your question put me in an awkward position. Left to myself, I should not have continued beyond the preliminary exposition of my new insight. To me that was enough, you know, and beyond that I had to some extent, as you rightly said, to strain intellectually, which is not really my nature at all. The essential thing for me was what I call the organic inter-linking of these two processes, and if I have to pick out one idea from all the rather laboured statements and attempts to state the nature of the inter-linking which followed later, it is the fact that in my experience we are here ultimately involved in an act of creation. And you may remember that this is what Jung said. I didn't say it because Jung had said it, but I'm extremely glad that he did say it. It's akin to the creative act of the artist, because, you see, the changes which take place can be so rapid and so surprising that you have to be completely adaptable, so to say, in a state of creativity, adjusting to what comes towards you, understanding it, and taking it a step further, although you may be totally unprepared for it. And what I am saying is that this state of creativity can only be achieved through two things: on the one hand, by allowing the purely structural elements of the counselling process to sink into the subconscious or even unconscious, and, on the other hand, by following and living in the spiritual path daily, for then, ideally, at least, you should have contact with something — I overstate it now, please — with something like an inflowing spirit, you know, which will keep you going and enable you to overcome the obstacles, to untie the knots, to recover from surprises, without being completely thrown. In other words, the process will flow, it will be alive, this is essentially what I meant.'

'Yes, I understand that very well, Martin, but you see what I'm concerned with is really to see more precisely what it is you're saying. I think that this insight into the inter-action between the two processes of counselling and the spiritual life is a most important one. In fact it's because it is so important that it's worth trying to disengage its nature as clearly as possible. I see further that what you're trying to do is to articulate very consciously something that goes on more or less unconsciously in any good act of communication, at any level. And I suspect that some such process goes on not only in the case of counselling but in the case of the musicians whom you have quoted to me before, or even, I suppose, in the act of sexual love-making.'

'Absolutely', concurred Dr. Gregory.

'There seems to be a common element in all such acts of communication. And I think that it is extremely important to try to express, define, formulate what it is that is going on because this is, I believe, largely unexplored territory — not the *fact* of what is going on, but what is *said* to be going on, and I think that you have expressed a great deal of what's going on, very, very well. But I should really like to go back to concentrating on two aspects of this, yes? On the one hand, critically, on what stage of the counselling process corresponds to what stage of the spiritual life; on the other hand, more constructively, on drawing out some of the implications of a more exact statement of your insight a little further. So I wish to take your thesis both backwards and forwards.'

'Yes, please do. Continue', said Dr. Gregory.

'Well, then, I'm thinking aloud, Martin. But, especially in the last bit, where you were trying once again to link the seven stages of counselling more precisely, point by point, to the four stages of spiritual development and consciousness, I had certain misgivings, and I can perhaps make them clear by summarising your argument in the form of a simple chart. The seven stages of the organic process of counselling seem in your mind to be correlative to the four stages of the organic process of spiritual growth in the following fashion:

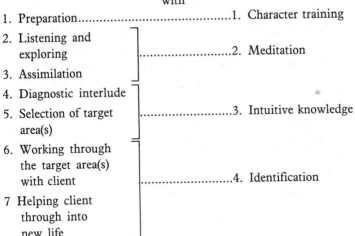

Stages of counselling

Stages of the spiritual life

can be correlated with

1. Preparation................................1. Character training

2. Listening and exploring
3. Assimilation
................Meditation

4. Diagnostic interlude
5. Selection of target area(s)
................3. Intuitive knowledge

6. Working through the target area(s) with client
7 Helping client through into new life
................4. Identification

Would you agree to this diagramatic way of recapitulating your thinking, Martin?'

'Yes, though subject to the reservation about the essentially creative nature of both processes, in themselves and in their interaction, that I have already expressed.'

'I accept that, Martin, but if you in your turn accept my summary, then it seems to me that on the negative and critical side of my response to you, this summary throws three difficulties into relief. In the first place, I'm not happy about your correlating the stage of assimilation to meditation, since the task of assimilation above all would seem to me to call for the deepest degree of awareness which you call intuitive knowledge, even identification. Then, secondly, I agree that it is again at this stage of assimilation that the what I shall now call discursive intellect most needs to be subdued in favour of the intuitive, almost subconscious, intellect, and yet, even on your own account, this same discursive intellect needs to be brought back into play for the purpose of the "diagnosis" (Stage 4), let alone for the purpose of the selection of the target area(s) (your Stage 5).'

'May I interrupt you for a moment on this last point, Marcus? You are, of course, quite right to say that the more conscious mind partly re-emerges at these stages of the counselling process. But I tried to allow for this by saying that at the stages of the "diagnostic interlude" and of the selection of the target area(s) (and the subsequent stages too for that matter) "intuitive knowledge" is not the only function but one that aids the conscious function: the intuitive intellect as it were backs up the conscious mind.'

'Yes, I understand now', I replied. 'But that still leaves me with my third and main difficulty here. You speak so well about the need to identify with the other that you seem, at least to me, to fail to do justice to the fact that the counsellor nevertheless *also* remains himself, for the fact that the counsellor remains himself is essential to his being able to work through the target area(s) with his client and to help him to establish himself in his new life, the final stages of the counselling process. You see, what interests me is not only the nature of the interaction between the two people, including the possibility of identification, but the very fact that there are two people for there to be an interaction between and who themselves therefore also remain themselves. And here I want to go on to the second, more constructive part of my embryonic reflection on your thesis, and that is: What is the most accurate, the best, the most adequate way of describing what is going on? You talk in terms of becoming the other, very finely and intuitively becoming the other, almost at the expense of, to the loss of, oneself. But in fact one does not disappear, as is proved by the fact that one re-emerges, and it is essential that one does so. So what precisely is going on? It is an identification with the other *without a loss of the self.* In fact one's continuing to be there and to be oneself, albeit in reserve, as it were, is vital for the other person, not only for the obvious reason that one has to be a guide, but for the more fundamental reason that one has to make it possible for the other, the client, as I put it before, to go out of his own world into another's, in this case the counsellor's. I think that this is as it were the alchemy of the thing.'

'Yes', Dr. Gregory nodded.

'I've been thinking a little more about all this myself. And to expand the use of this metaphor a little more, I think that the alchemy consists, on the one hand, in one person, the counsellor, being able to enter into the world of somebody who is living more or less in "a world of his own", as we say, and that's where the identification comes in. On the other hand, the very fact that one is able to do this, even before one does or even says anything, communicates itself to the other and is already incipiently liberating in so far as the other thereby begins to catch the sense of one's own world in the sort of way in which one has been able to catch a sense of his and he can therefore begin to enlarge and correct his hitherto restrictive world. But, if that's in any way true, then it means that there are always two present, you see, so that talk of the dissolution of the self or anything that suggests that, is strictly inaccurate.'

'But I didn't say that the counsellor somehow dissolves', protested Dr. Gregory.

'No, you didn't, not quite, but I think you very much underemphasised yourself, because you were so concerned with becoming the other — "I felt him","I felt...identified with him", "I suddenly knew what it was and how it was to be him at the moment", subject to all his stresses and strains as if they were your own, you said.'

'May I interrupt here for a moment? I do follow you, and I don't want to interrupt for long, because you have, with great subtlety and perceptiveness, taken the analysis much further than I have or could have done, because, you know, I haven't that sort of mind. But once you put it like that to me, I see that you are quite right. Even when I say I identify and speak of total assimilation, I do retain my sense of self, there are two of us.'

'But I think that this is very important for the accuracy of the description of what's going on. Because I think that if one didn't insist on this one could all too easily slip into an Eastern type of sense of the dissolution of the self. And this is where I think that the second, more constructive part of my incipient critique of your thesis really comes in.

You see, what I'm saying is that there are two present all the time, interacting in an extraordinarily sensitive and subtle way. But I wonder whether that's all there is to it, and whether the very perception of this fact doesn't carry us further. What I'm feeling for is something suggested by a term that came into my head as I was coming here this morning, Martin, in expectation of our continued dialogue today. It's a very suggestive term. It's a term that was first used by the Greek Fathers of the fourth century about the inter-relationships within the Trinity: *perichoresis*. It means, literally, the proceeding around each other, and it's the sort of dance of reciprocal identifications with each other in abiding distinctness that the Fathers call *perichoresis*. The Latin Fathers called it *circumincession:* the going into and around each other within a kind of circle of communication between the persons of the Trinity. And my hunch is that the same sort of thing is somehow going on within a counselling relationship, or more deeply, any true *Gespräch*. Paradoxically, then, I think that this theological, supernatural term is perhaps the best term with which to hit off the intricacies of the reciprocal identification and interacting identities between two human beings. But, by the same token, and also by the token of what you yourself have said, even when one is apparently by oneself, practising as best one can, in all humility, the spiritual life, there is, as you said, the sense of the inflowing of the Spirit. So I wonder whether, *alike* in one own's personal meditation and in any communication with another, there are in fact always not simply two but somehow three persons present: there is the other — human being — either explicitly or implicitly, but also the Other, with a capital "O".'

'I couldn't agree more', Dr. Gregory interposed. 'That's very beautiful, what you say about the *perichoresis* — is that the right word?'

'Yes'

'This is what I felt but could not formulate like that. It's what I, perhaps very inadequately, implied with the quotation from Goethe. For in what he refers to as *Gestaltung, Umgestaltung,* you have the element of movement, of flux, therefore of finding and losing, everything that you have indicated in your term *perichoresis* and your talk of the 'dance', almost the cosmic dance, contained therein. But what you have also indicated — and I am most grateful for this too — is something else that I have been conscious of in a penumbral way and then become centrally aware of as you challenged me, and this is that the Other with a capital "O" is present. But then, even here, Goethe can be said to have pointed the way, in so far as, after the *Gestaltung, Umgestaltung,* he goes on to mention what can be taken to refer to that influx of the living spirit which comes from above, therefore from the Other. And there you have it all, only I could never in my life have expressed it like that by myself. So here again, as far as our own relationship is concerned, we are, if I may say so, acting out the *Urphänomen* that we two function at different levels; I function at the level of simple experience, whilst you function at a more analytic level. The difference as well as the mutual responsiveness is amazing, but, quite frankly, I don't think that there is any contradiction between us in all this.'

'No, Martin, there's not', I agreed.

'You have just refined and expressed what I had said in a much more, well, spiritualised form and thereby immensely enriched the whole thing, that's what it is.'

'Well, that's a very generous way of talking about an exchange in which I persist in thinking you have in fact had the really seminal ideas. But, emboldened by your remarks, may I now just dot a few "i's" and cross a few "t's"? I think that through struggling with your ideas — or perhaps I should say, through entering more intensely into your struggle with your own ideas — I can now see a little more clearly how I should reformulate this major insight of yours. The apparently negative part of my criticism of your thesis is very much subordinate to the more positive part of it, namely, the reformulation of your insight in such a way as to enable us to see further implications of it. I think that what I'm trying to say is that I cetainly want to affirm your central insight about what you call the inter-linking of the stages of the counselling process with the stages of spiritual development, since it is most valuable, but I also want to locate them more precisely in relation to each other, if at all possible, and so be able to take your insight further. For if I'm right in thinking that the different stages of awareness are interfused with different stages of any true communication more variously and more subtly than you seemed to state in the reformulation of your initial insight, then I think that we can restate my own central idea of the *perichoresis* — which is a reformulation of your central idea! — in another way. We can say, can't we, that precisely because there is this *perichoresis*, this alternating response and successive interaction of two people in the sustaining presence of the Other, a Third, in the *Umwelt*, in this enveloping ambience, if you like, of the *ewigen Sinn*, eternal meaning and its *ewige Unterhaltung*, its eternal upholding, then the different stages of spiritual development represent various aspects or levels of the circling or spiralling of communication. They represent as it were the rising and falling, of, well, the conscious self of now one, now the other, as well as of the reasoning self as distinct from the intuitive self of one *within* himself, so that there is — it's very difficult to describe — something like a wave motion, there's a rhythm, an undulation and a rhythm of alternation and balancing, yes, of some dance between the two, but also of some dance *within* each one.'

'Yes, very beautiful, Marcus', Dr. Gregory said. 'And again you used a cosmic image; you used the image of flux, of motion, of the tide, of *Gestaltung, Umgestaltung*. So here I want to come back to what for me is the essential thing from a practical point of view. So far we have been thinking — *I* have been thinking — that there is a counselling process on the one hand and there is a spiritual life on the other, so that you can be a good counsellor — or you can try to be a good counsellor — in one part of your life, and in another part of your life you can go along the spiritual path in order to become a well — or more — balanced and perhaps a slightly more spiritualised human being. But I had never before experienced with such immediacy that there is a complete interaction. In other words, if somebody wants to be a counsellor in the sense we have been discussing this, then there is really so intimate an interplay between the processes of counselling and the spiritual life that it is necessary *not only* to give a counsellor, say, a training analysis, which is very good, or supervision over a period of time, *but also* to give him a spiritual training — and not only a spiritual training in order to make him a better, a more balanced, a more orientated person in himself, but also to give him the possibility of being *a better counsellor* who will function in the very counselling situation with much greater perceptiveness, and with much better judgment. That is my main point.'

'Yes, I quite agree with that, Martin, and I think that it is for this reason that I should again slightly reformulate one of your other important statements, namely that the spiritual life can become the manifestation of the archetype of true relationship. I think that I should put it slightly differently and start by recurring to another reference of yours to Goethe. According to you, Goethe speaks of man being *der dialogische Mensch* — a creature capable of and constituted by dialogue. *Gespräch* or dialogue is the archetype of which counselling is one expression because man is in his innermost being a *dialogische Mensch,* a dialogical being. It's because man is a *dialogische Mensch* that he carries on dialogues.'

'May I say "should be"?', said Dr. Gregory.

'Well, should be and therefore in some profound sense by nature is, a being of dialogue. In his innermost being, he is capable of dialogue, however overgrown or stunted this capacity may be. And it follows that the tearing, the losing of the centre which you began by speaking about can then be defined as an impairment of this innermost nature. What, then, is the innermost nature of this *Gespräch,* this dialogue? Let's take this a bit further. Well, the *Gespräch* is with a human partner in dialogue and so has an evident human dimension. But we have also begun to glimpse that every true dialogue seems in its depths to carry a reference to a third person and to have another dimension, the dimension of the Other. At the same time, we have between us also glimpsed that the goal of the spiritual life is union with the Other, which union, however, also liberates us for deeper communion with other human beings. The discipline of the spiritual life therefore carries a reference to fellow human beings, to the human dimension. It seems to me, therefore, that the human dialogue (whether in the form of counselling or otherwise) is as it were the becoming explicit, the externalisation of the spiritual life, and vice-versa. The dialogue and the practice of the spiritual life differ in that the dialogue makes evident the human aspect of the triadic relationship of, shall we now say I — thou — Thou/we, whereas the practice of the so-called spiritual life makes evident the divine aspect. In this perspective, then, dialogue and spirituality become as it were the two faces of the same reality, the one the more overtly human face, the other the more overtly spiritual face; or the outwardness and the inwardness of the same thing. So I conclude with you that the proceses of counselling and of the spiritual life are indeed indissolubly united, but I do so in a somewhat different way from you. Do you see?'

'I do indeed', responded Dr. Gregory warmly, 'and I quite agree with that way of seeing it too. In that regard, I should just like to add something which has recently come to me. I was reading the gospel of St. John again not so long ago and there I came upon that passage where Jesus is reported as saying — and again I'll say it first in German: *"Wer aufnimmt den ich gesandt habe, der nimmt mich auf, und wer mich aufnimmt . . ."* You understand: "He who receives the one I have sent also receives me, and he who receives me . . ." Now as I read this, it occurred to me that this expressed exactly what happens at a sort of mystical — is that the right word? — level in a *Gespräch*. You take into yourself, you take *auf*, somebody whom destiny, life itself has sent you, but the moment you do that you take on, *auf*, the Other, you follow me? We are back to what you just said. In other words, if you think of the *Gespräch*, the listening, as an *Aufnehmen*, an interiorisation or assimilation, then the moment you truly and devotedly and humbly and lovingly do that, then you take *auf*, you accept, you receive someone who has been sent to you, and, by doing so, Him who has sent that person. Do you follow me? Does that relate?'

'Yes, indeed', I replied, 'it's the same trinity, if you like'.

'Yes, the same trinity', Dr. Gregory confirmed.

'It's the mystery of the inter-relationship between one's fellow-men and God: God is in the other and yet is more than the other, he is other than the other.'

'Yes. And when I came across this passage, it occured to me to say to a friend who is coming up to see me to ask: "What is a *Gespräch*, a dialogue?", "Well, in the first place it is a mystery" .'

'I don't think there's any more to say', I said. 'Or else there's still so much to say. Besides, it's almost time for me to go.'

'Shall we switch off then?', Dr. Gregory asked.

dialogue 7: the open end

The announcement of another dialogue followed by a largely blank page is more than a trick; it is a symbol. The absence of a further dialogue is only apparent. The void is what the Japanese would call plenary. The white open space suggests the dialogues continued between Dr. Gregory and myself, or within ourselves, or with others. It is thus the expression in type of the Zen Buddhist notion of the return to the market place of ordinary life once the oxen have been herded and caught. It is only once you have something that you can give it. The blank is thus, variously, the symbol of continuation; of return to contact with others who are in turn in contact with yet others; of the recycling and circulation of ideas and life energy; of the progressive inwardness of all this; but therefore and through it all of that final liberation to which Dr. Gregory alluded in Dialogue 5: *Der Geist wird frei,* the spirit becomes free.

epilogue

From the very beginning I have tried to make it clear, on the one hand, that in my opinion the really creative ideas emerged from my friend Dr. Gregory and his long and deeply pondered experience of counselling, however much the very potency of his ideas may then have stimulated me to respond at every level of my being, and, on the other, that the script sought to retain as much of the liveliness but therefore also something of the inchoateness of any such dialogue. The dialogues shared here represent essentially unfinished as well as unpolished business. It is to this aspect of them that I should like to recur here by way of an epilogue and write a few concluding words in my own voice alone in virtue of my privilege as editor, as the person who has taken the liberty of making certain changes to the original tapes, though in the spirit of bringing out the inherent shape and flow of these conversations rather than of imposing anything new on them.

If the dialogues as we have arranged them and as I have edited them seem to have some organic sequence and direction, this is not because we had planned them like that. We did in the end have the benefit of hindsight and we could discuss our progress as we went along, but basically we allowed one topic to suggest another and in this way the succeeding one to grow out of the one that had gone before, just as each individual dialogue developed it's own vital sinuousities — some of our readers may well think too many or too self-indulgently! The very process of our conversations over some four years did not, therefore, allow us to make every theme explicit; there was too much exploration, emergence, discovery going on, and this through our very responsiveness to each other. And it is the presence of many such only part explicitated, only part enunciated threads or potencies that Chapter 7, 'The Open End' represents and symbolises. One such semi-emergent theme I should, however, like to hew out a little more, though even that will no doubt remain as unfinished as — to invoke a mighty precedent — Michelangelo's Rondanini pietà.

This theme, as I now reflect upon the course of our conversations, seems in retrospect to be like a veritable leitmotif. First introduced so piano as to be almost inaudible, it is then alluded to at various moments but then again allowed to recede until it finally gathers to something more like a stronger crescendo in the penultimate dialogue, on the inter-relationship between the stages of counselling and the stages of the spiritual life. This theme is the theme of the half-glimpsed, half-hiding, the elusive, the thus almost playful, in this sense Pan-like presence of what we called the Other, between, in the midst of and around the two in their mutual otherness.

Now I fully realise that many of our readers who may well have been with us sympathetically until this moment may at this point leave us with varying degrees of derision and sadness. I should, however, like to suggest that the deeper one allows oneself to go into a relationship and into the reflective awareness of such a relationship, the more the mystery of it all discloses itself as the mysterious presence of some third thing that is so subtle, sensitive and quickening as to be somehow personal, a breath, a breathing that is like an inspiration as well as a grace. Such, I venture to submit, is what is revealed in the very depths, the innermost core or cave of such an experience of dialogue and reciprocal duality. This is, in Dr. Winifred Rushforth's fine phrase, the truth at the bottom of the well — the unfailing source of the source, the mystery underlying the wellspring. And this, then, is the inner explanation of the terms of the sub-title we have chosen for these conversations: dialogue and trinity. They represent the inner élan or thrust of these conversations as it gradually unfolded itself, at least to me: counselling undertaken with the love that is nourished by a sincere spiritual life gradually reveals itself to be, as Dr. Gregory puts it, a manifestation of some archetype of dialogue, which itself however, in its turn reveals itself as the human figure of some more eternal face-to-face.

These concluding thoughts are, therefore, highly personal. At the same time I do not think that they are entirely idiosyncratic. And in order to suggest that we are here, in Jung's evocative phrase, 'circumambulating about an unknown centre' in the company of some not undistinguished men down the ages, I want to end with two quotations. They are from two seers who happen to represent the two traditions which my friend Dr. Gregory and I also represent in our little way, the Judaic and the Catholic. The first comes from Martin Büber:

> Every particular *Thou* is a glimpse through to the eternal *Thou;* by means of every particular *Thou* the primary word addresses the eternal *Thou.* Through this mediation of the *Thou* of all beings fulfilment, and non-fulfilment, of relations comes to them: the inborn *Thou* is realised in each relation and consummated in none. It is consummated only in the direct relation with the *Thou* that by its nature cannot become *It.*[1]

The second quotation comes from St. Thomas Aquinas.

> "Taken as a personal name, 'Gift' is proper to the Holy Spirit. To understand why, reflect that a gift, according to Aristotle, is literally a giving that can have no return, that is to say it is not given with repayment in mind and as such denotes a giving out of good will. Now the basis for such gracious giving is love; the reason why we give something to another spontaneously is that we want good for him. And so what we give first to anyone is the love itself with which we love him. Clearly, then, love has the quality of being our first gift; through love we give all other loving gifts (*amor habet rationem primi doni per quod omnia dona gratuita donantur*). Since, then, as shown, the Holy Spirit comes forth as Love, he proceeds as being the first Gift. So St. Augustine teaches that "through the Gift who is the Holy Spirit, the many individuals gifts are distributed to Christ's members."[2]

'Every particular *Thou* is a glimpse through to the eternal *Thou.*' 'Through love we give all other loving gifts.'

notes

1. Martin Büber *I and Thou,* (T. & T. Clark, Edinburgh, 1959), at p.75.
2. St. Thomas Aquinas, *Summa Theologica* Ia. Q.38, art.2; c.1265; Vol.7 of the bilingual edition, (Eyre & Spottiswoode, 1976), at p.95.

Books referred to:

Anselm of Canterbury (1033-1109), *Cur Deus Homo*

Aquinas, Thomas (1225-1274) *Summa Theologica*, Eyre and Spottiswode, London, 1976

Beckh, H. *Buddha und seine Lehre*, Verlag Urachhaus, Stuttgart 1958

Beckh, H. *Der Hingang des Vollendeten*, Verlag Urachhaus, Stuttgart 1960

Brown, D. and Pedder, J. *Introduction to Psychotherapy*, Tavistock Publications, London 1979

Buber, M. *I and Thou*, T & T Clark, Edinburgh 1959

Cox, M. *Coding the Therapeutic Process: Emblems of Encounter*, Pergamon Press, Oxford 1978

Dante (1265-1321) *La Divina Commedia*, Oxford University Press, London, 1971

Goethe, J.W. von (1749-1832) *Das Märchen*, Deutscher Taschenbuch Verlag, Munich, 1968

Goethe, J.W. von *Wilhelm Meister's Lehrjahre*, Deutsher Taschenbuch Verlag, Munich, 1968

Goethe, J.W. von *Faust*, Deutscher Taschenbuch Verlag, Munich, 1968

Goleman, D. *Varieties of Meditative Experience*, London 1978

Harding, E. *The Way of All Women*, Rider, New York 1971

Jacobi, J. *Jung, Psychological Reflections*, Pantheon Books Inc., New York 1953

Lewis, C.S. *The Four Loves*, Fontana, London 1963

Lotz, J.B. *Erfahrungen mit der Einsamkeit*, Herder, Freiburg-im-Breisgau, 1972

Macmurray, J. *Persons in Relation*, Faber & Faber, London, 1961

Plato (427-347 B.C.) *The Symposium*

Radhakrishnan *Indian Philosophy*, Vols. I and II, Allen and Unwin, London, 1923-27

Reiter, U. *Meditation — Wege zum Selbst* Mosaik Verlag, Munich 1976

Rilke, R.M. (1872-1928), *Briefe an einen jungen Dichter*, Insel Verlay, Frankfurt-am-Main, 1955

Rilke, R.M. *Duineser Elegien*, Insel Verlag, Frankfurt-am-Main, 1955

Stafford-Clark, D. *Psychiatry for Students,* Allen and Unwin, London 1979

Steiner, R. *Knowledge of the Higher Worlds and its Attainment,* Anthroposophic Press, New York 1947

Steiner, R. *Practical Training in Thought,* Anthroposophic Press, New York, 1948.

Storr, A. *The Art of Psychotherapy,* Secker & Warburg/Heinemann, London, 1979

Thomas à Kempis (c.1380-1471) *De Imitatione Christi*

Underhill, E. *Mysticism,* Methuen, London, 1904.

Whistler, L. *The Initials in the Heart,* Rupert Hart-Davis, London, 1966

Wiegand, H.J. (Ed.) *Goethe: Wisdom and Experience,* Routledge and Kegan Paul, London, 1949.

Zaehner, R.C. *Hindu Scriptures,* J.M. Dent & Sons, London, 1966

Zweig, S. *Die Welt von Gestern,* Fischer Taschenbuch, Berlin & Frankfurt-am-Main 1965.

Date Due